SEÁN TREACY
AND THE
TAN WAR

Seán Treacy
and the
Tan War

Joe Ambrose

MERCIER PRESS

WHAT YOU NEED TO READ

MERCIER PRESS
Douglas Village, Cork
www. mercierpress. ie

Trade enquiries to CMD Distribution
55A Spruce Avenue, Stillorgan Industrial Park,
Blackrock, County Dublin

© Joe Ambrose, 2007

ISBN: 978 1 85635 554 4

10 9 8 7 6 5 4 3 2 1

A CIP record for this title is available from the British Library

Mercier Press receives financial assistance from
the Arts Council/An Chomhairle Ealaíon

Printed and bound by J.H. Haynes & Co. Ltd, Sparkford.

CONTENTS

MAP OF CO. TIPPERARY

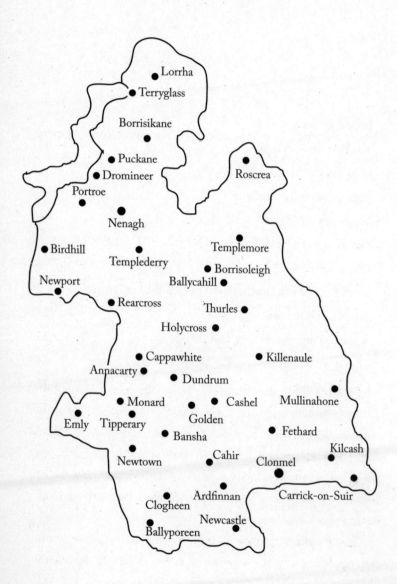

INTRODUCTION

This is the story of how a colonial power went from enjoying its self-image as a paternal benefactor looking after the interests of those who couldn't look after themselves, to being called 'the enemy' by a community it had previously seen through slightly comic, Somerville and Ross-style, rose tinted glasses. This is a story about how a revolutionary organisation, one which incorrectly believed that there was a 'little spark of nationality' in each Irish heart, forced a colonial power to leave its territory.

The process kicked off in Tipperary in the late 1840s when Ireland was ravaged by famine. The Tipperary part of the story concluded in the early 1920s when the last British soldiers left that county.

One of the people who turned the woolly romanticism of the Young Irelanders and the Fenians into an authentic revolutionary force on the ground in Tipperary was Seán Treacy. One of Treacy's comrades said that he was, 'a man who knew precisely what he was doing and why he was doing it.' This self-knowledge characterised Ireland's revolutionary generation and made their IRA a hard-nosed remorseless foe.

The revisionist historian Roy Foster has suggested that cosmopolitanism is the opposite of nationalism, but the women and men who adopted a nationalist stance during the Tan War were the very essence of political sophistication. They identified an intractable predicament – the British colonial presence in their country – and they resolved that problem.

Reading through the Witness Statements which the Tipperary veterans of the Tan War gave to the Bureau of Military History* between 1947 and 1957, one comes across repeated references to the fact that the witnesses involved – by then middle-aged or approaching old age – wanted their accounts of war to be written down and filed away for the benefit of future historians. Such declarations seem terribly poignant today as I read the carbon copies of their efforts in Dublin's National Archive before walking out into the optimistic sunshine of contemporary Ireland. The contradictory blend of idealism, realism and bloody-mindedness which informed those veterans' actions during their war also informed their testimonies. The naïve sense of civic duty which brought about their participation in the war, and their subsequent co-operation with the Bureau of Military History, is entirely alien to the acquisitive money-orientated consensus which defines the Ireland of today. Their keen engagement with the Bureau was inherently sophisticated, as were their hardboiled, unadorned statements.

Many of them made it clear that the events they were talking about had happened long ago and that their recollections might, therefore, be deficient or imprecise. They remembered as best they could and the impressive thing about their collective testimonies is the fact that, in most cases, their narratives neatly dovetail with one another. This gives their assertions a certain integrity and dependability. In one or two cases – where different witnesses use almost identical turns of phrase and excuses for actions – the men and women involved had clearly rehearsed, between themselves, what they were going to say. Such duplications represent a miniscule percentage of the whole.

By the time their stories were collected, many of these people had long abandoned their unassuming youthful rural lifestyles in favour of middle-aged bourgeois comforts and were resident in some of the nicer parts of Dublin, beneficiaries of the Ireland they had helped create. Others stayed down the country, working the farms or businesses they had inherited from their fathers. Still others moved from the land into the big towns in the county such as Clonmel and Nenagh.

They hoped that – as a result of their taking time out to reminisce about events which had played out thirty or forty years before – their actions and motivations would be better understood at a time and in a place which was essentially inconceivable to them, since none of us can really identify with a future world in which we will no longer exist.

The result of the Bureau's activities is an unprecedented meat, potatoes, and two veg narrative concerning the evolution of an insurrection and revolution. It is just as well that those people took the opportunity to set the record straight because a lot of time, money and oblique energy has since been put into setting the record crooked.

Contemporary academic historians scrutinising the war have tended to reject traditional narrative history in favour of a rather tedious statistically-based analysis and high-falutin jargon. Such a methodology conveniently downplays exciting legends, implications of daring, and any sense one might get of plucky rural communities taking on a powerful global empire. The conclusions consistently drawn from this sort of research – undertaken by people like Foster, Peter Hart and Joost Augusteijn – tend to suggest that the War of Independence IRA didn't enjoy the support of the entire population. This conclusion isn't exactly rocket science; one doesn't need to do years of painstaking heavily-funded research to prove that violent revolutions are never universally popular. Most decent people favour peace and quiet over violence and trouble. The need to assert, repeatedly, that the IRA was not unanimously loved serves an entirely political but unhistorical purpose. The unspoken implication is that, since their actions were not always popular, what the IRA was doing was morally wrong. Whether they *were* morally right or wrong is a subject which deserves to be addressed directly, not at an angle. This book attempts to do so.

The motivations which underpin past wars and campaigns of coercion entered into by states and empires are rarely subjected to the same forensic examination which now stalks our collective remembrance of the Tan War. The mandate of the state is deemed sufficient moral authority for any belligerence. Consequently, today, we have 'peacekeeping forces' being sent by the 'international community' to inflict 'democracy' on vast unwilling swathes of humanity.

Academic reliance on state papers to plot the evolution of the Tan War serves the same contemporary political purpose as the statistical approach. The correspondence and reports penned by policemen, civil administrators, spies and representatives of the British establishment are cheerfully accepted as if this occasional 'parcel of rogues' were men of inherent integrity. It is intellectually comfortable to make value judgments which conclude that such sources are reliable. Most academics are cheerleaders for, and employees of, the state. Writing the history of revolutionary organisations and individuals requires a psychological grasp of the revolutionary spirit and process which is anathema to academic thinking and lifestyle. This book attempts to take on board the emotional landscape within which the War of Independence came about.

The rejection of narrative history – best exemplified by Richard English's dull study of Ernie O'Malley – is symptomatic of the disservice being done to the writing of Irish history by university-employed historians. The notion that history is a branch of literature has been jettisoned in favour of a pseudo-scientific academic style and approach which serves the purposes of inept over-excited non-entities.

The story of the long-ago and important war which started in Tipperary can't be left in the hands of such people. Neither can we rely on the braggadocio of the 'party line' post-colonial memoirs and histories (by the likes of Dan Breen, Tom Barry and Desmond Ryan) which tell the story in a more traditional way. The books those people wrote served another, inspirational, political purpose. Proud of the achievements of the revolutionary generation, they wrote it like they saw it. Their books captured the spirit of a 'nation' which was partially very real and partially an imaginative construct with roots in Fenianisn.

This book is the story of the violent attempt that a substantial section of Irish society made to bridge the gap between their ideals and the actual world in which they lived and died.

Joe Ambrose
www.joeambrose.net

1

THE PREMIER COUNTY?

The troops live not on earth could stand
The headlong charge of Tipperary.

Thomas Davis

'Where Tipperary leads, Ireland follows,' wrote John Mitchel, the Young Ireland propagandist and intellectual. Mitchel had such faith in that county's innate rebelliousness that he also called it the Premier County and, along with his Young Irelander pals, hoped that it was a place from which the momentum needed to drive the British out of Ireland would come.

They imagined that Tipperary was special because it had a long tradition of social and land disturbances most recently manifested in the Whiteboy* and Ribbonmen* agitations. For Mitchel's romantic and idealistic comrades, the county seemed to be a lofty spot full of noble souls imbued with a pure and ancient sense of separateness from Britain.

Was Tipperary unique, was it in thrall to a vision of freedom, and did it make a notable contribution to the eventual fight for independence?

Cultural commentator Michael Murphy thinks that Tipperary *was* different from other parts of Ireland. 'It comes as no surprise to discover that the county played an inordinate role in many Irish Ireland or separatist campaigns,' he says. 'When one thinks of what constitutes the idea – or the ideal – of "Ireland" one is really thinking about Tipperary, Limerick, Cork and Kerry. Those counties played inordinately significant roles, over the last two centuries, in the resistance to British rule. Tipperary has the rural landscape and the tone of voice which we think about when we think about "Ireland". They have a great sense of identity down there. Places like Tipperary or north Cork are prosperous enough, and far enough away from the British influence, to have a self-confident sense of culture and identity. People there are pretty determined and assertive.'

Land and the relationship with the land was always a substantial part of the Tipperary psyche. Mountains – and mountain people – played their part. The Comeraghs and Galtees were good fighting, hiding, and escaping terrain. The people who lived in those hills, like hill people everywhere, had an air of independence about them.

Down on the plains there was good land on which a lot of people lived in relative comfort. Nancy Mitford, at one time a regular visitor to Fethard, commented on the quality of the land and the ease which this brought into the lives of the people. In *The Other Island* she wrote: 'The plane of Tipperary is the richest farm land in western Europe, so fertile that farming there requires little skill; beasts are simply left in the fields until they are fat enough to be sold. It is beautiful beyond words and empty.'

There was, however, a bit more to farming than sitting about watching the cattle or the horses growing up. 'There was a love of discussion,' IRA leader Ernie O'Malley wrote about country people, 'and argument that would take up a subject casually without belief and in a searching way develop it … Deferential to a stranger, they evoked in themselves a sympathetic mood, changing gears in conversation to suit his beliefs and half believing them through sympathy whilst he was present. Afterwards when they checked up on themselves it might be different; they would laugh at the stranger's outlandish opinions when their mood had hardened … The weekly market was a break in routine. The men were able to drink double or triple porter to their hearts' content. Then the boisterous drove home, often without lights, careering along the country roads in a bone-shaking cart. The countryman, to himself, was worth what he had in his pocket at any given moment. The land was his wealth; unlike the townsman, he had few ornate possessions. He would look with envy at the many knick-knacks and furniture of a town house. His total wealth would be greater, but his living was simpler. He had no useless possessions.'

Historian Joost Augusteijn, questioning whether or why Tipperary played such a significant role in the Tan War, wondered if the county's alleged uniqueness was due to its prosperity, its tradition of rebellion, or to a dependable local nationalist leadership over a long period of time.

In Augusteijn's essay debunking the myth of Tipperary as an innate hotbed of rebellion, *Why was Tipperary so Active in the War of Independence?* he asserts: 'Tipperary was indeed a county with a strong tradition of emigration and agrarian violence in the late nineteenth century, which seems to have established a greater willingness to oppose the authorities with force. The relatively high numbers of local police indicates the continued expectation of such unrest among the authorities … The big questions, however, remain; how did these elements predetermine Tipperary to violence, why was there early activity in Tipperary, and how did this early activity lead to the outbreak of high levels of conflict in 1920-21? … The correlation with agrarian agitation and emigration in the nineteenth century tells us little about those in Tipperary who became active in the War of Independence. It may have established some sort of radical tradition in which the use of force was an accepted form of political expression, one in which at least a part of the population was willing to acquiesce.'

Augusteijn looks to Tipperary's past agrarian extremism in his search for the roots of 'some sort of radical tradition' but neatly sidesteps the self-evident nineteenth century political legacy passed down from one generation to the next, which started with the Young Irelander clashes of 1848-9.

The Young Irelanders, sophisticated cosmopolitan writers and theorists, made their Francophile plans in the coffee houses of Dublin but they struck out for their principles in and around Tipperary's rainy streets and hills. Their romantic but unsuccessful agitations soon gave rise, seamlessly, to Fenianism, a covert political belief system which flourished in some Tipperary minds. From the ashes of Fenianism arose the revived twentieth century Irish Republican Brotherhood (IRB). Tipperary members of the IRB, styling themselves the Irish Republican Army (IRA), led the 1919 Soloheadbeg ambush which is usually credited with being the first engagement in the War of Independence.

The radical tradition which took advantage of Tipperary's forthright spirit first established itself in the county via the Young Irelanders.

A mass meeting of Irish Confederation supporters was held on Slievenamon mountain, just north of Carrick-on-Suir, on Sunday 16 July 1848. The Irish Confederation, the organisation within which the Young Irelanders operated, was a breakaway from Daniel O'Connell's ineffective Repeal movement. Repealers sought to undo the Act of Union* between Britain and Ireland by constitutional means. The Repeal strategy involved, in practice, operating in cahoots with the Whig faction in the London parliament. The Young Irelanders, mostly journalists and agitators from privileged backgrounds, provided O'Connell with intellectual backbone until, in the aftermath of the 1845 famine, they grew disillusioned with him and felt that a more extreme response was needed to the British presence in Ireland. Drawing inspiration from French revolutionary stances, these angry eager, young men sought to fundamentally alter the Irish situation.

Their trump card was their newspaper, *The Nation*, which enjoyed a large circulation and substantial influence.

Confederate Club members from Fethard, Carrick, Kilsheelan, Cashel, Clonmel, and Kilcash planned the Slievenamon mass meeting and chose that location because of its iconic status. *The Nation* saw the mountain as the epitome of Tipperary's alleged rebel heart. For the Young Irelanders, says Patrick C. Power in his *History of South Tipperary*, the county had, 'become a symbol of hardy resistance to British rule because of its rather violent history of faction-fighting and Whiteboy struggles'.

Slievenamon and the nearby village of Kilcash enjoyed both local and national symbolic prominence. Slievenamon's legend went back into the mists of Irish mythology. Folk singer Liam Clancy from the Clancy Brothers explains the mountain's exotic nature: 'It is shaped like a beautiful female breast and on its summit sits a cairn of stones, like a nipple. The name Slievenamon comes from the Gaelic, *Sliabh na mBan*, the mountain of the women ... Some say the mountain got its name from the profile it presents when seen from Carrick-on-Suir, the town in which I was born. A more intriguing story tells how the legendary giant Fionn McCool would need a new wife each year and, because of his mighty demands, would put all the candidates vying for the job to a test. On a certain day of the year they would all race to the top of Slievenamon and back. The winner, he considered, might have the stamina to cope with his virility for the next year.'

In the lead up to the Young Irelander Slievenamon gathering, the local authorities operating out of Carrick grew paranoid and anxious about the possibility of an actual insurrection taking place. The town's resident magistrate reported to Dublin Castle on 14 July that: 'This town Carrick is the very hot-bed of sedition. There are I understand twelve hundred persons connected with Clubs ... the leprous distilment of bad advice poured among them in every possible manner. If a rising broke out, the greater number of the inhabitants of this populous town will be found ready to enter upon any treasonable project, however fatuous and visionary it may be.'

Given the tense circumstances, a member of the Irish Constabulary was sent out to Slievenamon on the Sunday to gather evidence and intelligence at the gathering. In the early morning he reported back, Kilcash's catholic church's bell rang out, summoning protestors and indicating to strangers unfamiliar with the terrain in that part of the country exactly where the meeting was due to take place.

Future Fenian leader John O'Mahony, a gentleman farmer who lived nearby at Ballyneale, led a large crowd towards Slievenamon. These people marched in military formation but, significantly, no leader was seen to give them anything that could be construed as military orders or instructions. Because O'Mahony didn't give out any such instructions, he was not subsequently arrested when five other individuals were charged, the day after the meeting, with giving military commands.

Those arrests gave rise to a protest meeting in Carrick where one of the most able and famous of the Young Irelanders, Thomas Francis Meagher – known as Meagher of the Sword because of his fiery oratory – was the main attraction. The well educated Meagher, who spoke in an urbane style which caused some to question his 'Irishness', knew how to stir a crowd into rebellion. Commentators have suggested that his familial connections with that part of Tipperary were responsible for the district being the site of the entire Young Ireland rebellion.

The escalating subversive buzz within the nationalist community made the authorities tense and some minor local radical leaders were arrested. Rumours began to circulate which suggested that the Constabulary had arrested Meagher and Michael Doheny, the Young Irelander thought to have written poetry for *The Nation* under the pseudonym 'A Tipperary Man'. The Fethard-born Doheny, along with John O'Mahony, would eventually found the Fenian Brotherhood in the United States.

Rumour, a powerful force within society, fanned the flames of revolt. The only substantial media available to the people were newspapers and magazines which reported the news days or weeks after the events involved. It was often rumour, therefore, which dictated events on the ground in the towns and villages.

On 24 July William Smith O'Brien, one of the most prominent Young Irelanders, a man treated like a revolutionary leader, showed up in Carrick and indulged in local rabble rousing. Patrick C. Power writes that, 'he did not have the support of the leaders of the Confederate movement in the town, who were all men of property, and he hesitated before taking any irrevocable step.'

Approximately four hundred men, who were minded to march on Carrick, gathered in the nearby village of Ballyneale. Eighty of these men had firearms; others carried pikes or farm implements. The Ballyneale parish priest persuaded them to disperse, convincing them that Meagher and Doheny were not locked up.

Then Smith O'Brien and his companions went northwards to the village of Ballingarry where over five hundred men are said to have joined them. Barricades were erected and the people of Ireland were invited to rise up in open rebellion against the British. Apart from a few minor spats in Killenaule and Mullinahone, nothing much along those lines seemed to happen. When a group of Irish Constabulary men, withdrawing from Ballingarry under pressure, sought sanctuary at the Widow McCormack's house they were besieged by Smith O'Brien's forces.

Playwright Donagh MacDonagh wrote that Smith O'Brien and other Young Ireland leaders had, prior to making a stand at Ballingarry, been touring the famine-ravaged countryside urging people to be ready to rise up. They, 'passed through Kilkenny where they were told that reinforcements would be necessary, and then into Tipperary where they held enthusiastic meetings, which became rather less enthusiastic as time passed and the people, hungry and thirsty, found nothing to eat or drink. At Mullinahone

Smith O'Brien bought them some bread himself, but told them that in future they would have to provide for themselves and that he would requisition nothing from any man. They returned home faint with hunger. Gradually, the crowds which had been so great and which had cheered so loudly began to fade away, and when the Catholic clergy came among them begging them to return home, pointing out their utter unpreparedness, their lack of weapons, the ignorance of military tactics of their leaders, the utter lack of food, most of them forgot their warlike spirit. To the majority Smith O'Brien's name was completely unknown, but his danger of immediate arrest without cause shown, the old tradition of revolt, and the appeal to them to risk an honourable death in action rather than one by starvation in a corner of their cabins, appealed strongly to them, and those who remained were willing to risk everything under the leadership of the Young Irelanders. At Boulagh Commons, where he gathered the miners from the local coal mines about him, Smith O'Brien found many eager volunteers, some of them already armed, others prepared to fight with their mining tools or to use their technical skill in trenching the roads against the police and military. While the meeting was still going forward the police and military were approaching Ballingarry ... The police from Callan were first to arrive, long before their time, and when the miners saw them riding forward in the distance they hastily threw up a barricade expecting a sudden assault. The police, on the other hand, when they saw a hundred or so miners gathered on the spoil-banks being harangued by a number of strange gentlemen, were not at all anxious to provoke an engagement and made for a substantial farmhouse which they saw some distance away. This was the Widow MacCormack's farm. In they went, tumbling over one another in their haste, for the miners, when they saw their change of direction, had made a rush to reach the farmhouse before them.'

Smith O'Brien, a Protestant radical from Limerick, refused to fire on the house because the Constabulary trapped inside were holding the Widow MacCormack's five children as hostages. 'Glory be to God, Sir,' the Widow is reported to have said to Smith O'Brien, going down on her knees, 'You can't risk the lives of those little innocent children for the sake of a couple of Constabulary men!'

The miners and other rebels, little by little, gave up the fight and dispersed. Their leader escaped into in the adjacent countryside.

On 2 September the Carrick authorities reported that pike-handles were being prepared in the town and that fires on the surrounding hills suggested a rebellion. On 12 September rumours reached Carrick to the effect that a large body of rebels were close at hand and that the bell of Kilcash church had once again rung out to rally disaffected elements.

Barges on the River Suir which were due to sail from Carrick to Clonmel were delayed because it was feared that they might be captured by rebels or that their horses might be seized. One barge did undertake the perilous journey and was intercepted by men under the command of John O'Mahony who ordered the ferrymen to transport one hundred of his supporters. A police station was attacked. Six policemen in the station, assisted by reinforcements, held off the attackers, killing two of them.

Those were the only substantial incidents which took place in the whole of Ireland during the much vaunted rebellion of 1848. The Young Irelanders either disappeared or were arrested.

John O'Mahony went initially to Paris and subsequently to New York. Smith O'Brien was arrested at Thurles railway station on 5 August and was put on trial with several others at Clonmel on 21 September charged with 'marching with great force and violence' at Ballingarry, erecting obstructions, making a warlike attack and firing on the police. The Young Irelander 'false traitors' were sentenced to death.

The young John O'Leary from Tipperary town was one of the Young Irelander stragglers who gathered at the Wilderness, a remote spot just outside Clonmel, with a view to rescuing the men incarcerated in Clonmel jail.

Smith O'Brien and his companions were, much to their chagrin, reprieved. Plans were made to move them to Thurles when their captors became aware of the Wilderness plot. O'Leary vacillated about whether to attempt a rescue in Clonmel or to ambush the party taking Smith O'Brien to Thurles. Eventually O'Leary and sixteen other men were arrested at the Wilderness on the night of 8 November, 1848. They were treated leniently by the courts and received only short sentences.

When he got out of prison O'Leary travelled by boat to Carrick. There he met up with Phil Gray, one of the last important Young Irelanders still at large. These two set about organising a covert anti-British organisation, complete with an oath of loyalty and a commitment to ending the Act of Union. John O'Mahony, cowering in Paris, was very much in league with them on this conspiracy.

Gray and O'Leary, remorseless rebels, started selling daggers to their Tipperary followers. 'The boatmen on the Suir were very active in the new secret organisation,' writes Patrick C. Power. 'A bitter boatmen's strike on the Suir between Clonmel and Carrick was looked upon as the prelude to a rising ... The substance behind all this was that a council of three leaders was leading the secret society, which had now succeeded the [Confederate] Clubs, and had decided to stage a revolt.'

During June 1849 O'Leary played host to James Fintan Lalor, the first Irish radical to adopt a neo-socialist agenda, and to the Tipperary-connected Thomas Clarke Luby. Lalor and Luby lived for a time with O'Leary in his Tipperary town home. The three planned yet another optimistic rising for 16 September. This time the weather went against them and the only manifestation of rebellion was a skirmish at Cappaquin Co. Waterford.

Desmond Ryan wrote that, 'before it could get under way the mobilisation was crippled by the government drafting troops in force into Tipperary and Waterford. [Joseph] Brenan led an attack on a police barracks at Cappaquin, but had to call off the attack after several casualties on both sides. Lalor waited all night with a hundred and fifty men to attack Cashel, but had to abandon it when contingents from other districts failed to arrive. Many groups that turned out were too small or totally unarmed and had to be sent home. John O'Leary dismissed his fifty men at Garnacarty for this reason. Luby was arrested in Cashel and shortly afterwards released.'

James Connolly* said that the Young Irelanders had been handed 'revolutionary material' (by which he meant favourable circumstances) and that they were 'unfit to use' that material. The significance of all their coming and going was not that a serious blow had been struck against British rule in Ireland – if anything the case for armed resistance had been grievously undermined by the multiple comic opera-style fiascos. Nevertheless, a self-image of Tipperary was created wherein its rebels would never say die, would never lie down or back down, no matter how hopeless the odds. Equally significant was the fact that a covert oath-bound organisation, supported by the majority of the prospective Fenian leadership, was up and running in Tipperary a decade before the actual Fenian organisation came into existence.

2

BOLD FENIAN MEN

The heart of the country always goes out to the man who lives
and dies an unrepentant rebel.

John O'Leary

Fenianism's leaders were an odd, dark and gifted bunch. James
Stephens, Chief Organiser, was a long-winded, arrogant schemer,
ruthless and ultimately incompetent. T.W. Moody said that
Stephens had 'a genius for organising and for inspiring loyalty,
but had few of the other qualifications of a successful leader of
rebellion'. John O'Leary, in effect a trust fund kid, was a bibliophile
and a curiously modern man of refreshingly sophisticated opinions.
Michael Doheny was a troubled, idealistic, rough diamond on a
doomed trajectory. Charles J. Kickham, blind and half deaf, took
his place at every Irish hearth via the sentimental maudlin ballads
which he wrote and via his novel, *Knocknagow or the Homes of
Tipperary* (1879).

None was odder than the scholarly, passionate, perpetually
cash-strapped John O'Mahony who ended up in New York leading
a fixated life which resembled, in many ways, that of the heroin or
opium addict.

All of the aforementioned men, and other prominent Fenians besides, played some part in the abortive Young Ireland rebellions which took place in Tipperary in 1848 and 1849. Most of them were very young at the time. Only Michael Doheny, a middle-aged self-made barrister, had played a significant part in the Irish Confederacy.

Doheny was born near Fethard but, after many vicissitudes, eventually based himself in Cashel. While a law student in London he had grown sympathetic to Chartist* thinking. By January 1847 he, like the other Young Irelanders, had become totally disillusioned with Repeal. He worked with Smith O'Brien, Meagher, Terence Bellew McManus and Thomas Darcy McGee on bringing the Irish Confederation into existence.

He addressed the 1847 Holycross meeting at which James Fintan Lalor founded the Tipperary Tenant League. He was more sympathetic than other Young Irelanders to Lalor's leftist vision. Following the 1848 Paris uprising, Doheny addressed a Chartists rally at the Manchester Free Trade Hall. Soon afterwards, sharing a platform with Chartist leader Fergus O'Connor, he announced, 'I am an Irish Chartist'.

By May 1848 it was Doheny, along with Thomas Francis Meagher, who was addressing the gathered Young Irelander supporters on the slopes of Slievenamon. He told the crowd who had come together on that conspicuously sunny day: 'How proud I am at meeting so many of my school-fellows who are here today to shed their last drop of blood for their country.'

It would be fair to say that Doheny's real Homeric political adventure only started once his starry-eyed Young Irelander hopes had been dashed. His subsequent exciting journey is well known because he wrote a widely read book about it, *The Felon's Track* (1867).

After the Ballingarry debacle Doheny and John O'Mahony retreated to Fethard where they were looked after and hidden by sympathetic locals. Then they walked to Carrick-on-Suir, eventually crossing the Suir and heading for Rathgormack Co. Waterford where O'Mahony went his own way and Doheny was joined by James Stephens. These two proceeded to walk across Munster together, keeping one another company until they could escape from Ireland. Initially they headed for the Cistercian (Trappist) monastery at Mount Melleray, crossing over the mountains into Dungarvan. Unable to gain passage to England from that port, they trudged on towards Dunmanway in West Cork.

For two months Doheny, a well fed comfortably off barrister in his early forties, lived in the hills, leading the life of the outlaw rapparee. 'Our destination was Dunmanway,' Doheny wrote in *The Felon's Track*, 'near which a friend of mine lived, in whose house I hoped we might remain concealed, while means of escape would be procured somewhere among the western headlands. A short journey brought us to this house. My friend was absent, but daughters of his, whom I had not seen since childhood, recognised and welcomed us. We had then travelled 150 miles.'

At one stage the two fugitives, fearing imminent arrest, abandoned Dunmanway for Killarney. Outside the town they followed a mountain stream which led them into a remote valley before they crossed over a mountain summit and clambered downhill into Killarney.

Stephens, long after the event, wrote of their escapade crisscrossing Munster: 'I can never resist wondering at and admiring the heroic way he [Doheny] bore himself in the face of his difficulties and the hazardous stands we were forced to make and confront throughout that felon's track of ours. It was nothing for a young man like me, without wife or child, to have gone on my way singing; but that he, having a woman he loved, and an interesting family he adored, bore up as he did, as well, if not better than myself, raised him to a heroic level in my estimation.'

Stephens, who didn't always make his points succinctly or well, hit the nail on the head on this occasion. There was something oddly noble or gallant about Doheny during those days.

Back in Dunmanway, their escape was finally organised. Stephens got away first, heading to Paris via England. Ultimately Doheny was sent by boat to Bristol. From there he too headed for Paris, arriving on 4 October 1848. Stephens acted as Doheny's guide to the Parisian social whirl but, whereas Stephens took to Parisian bohemian life like a duck to water, Doheny was just passing through. When he was joined by his family he sailed from Le Havre, bound for New York City. After a turbulent voyage, they reached the city on 23 January 1849. Doheny soon got dug into Irish-American affairs and was admitted to the New York Bar. In 1855 he brought together, in his law offices, the men who founded the Fenian Brotherhood. Doheny, Michael Corcoran and John O'Mahony were the Brotherhood's earliest leading lights in New York.

Before O'Mahony headed for permanent and lonely exile in New York, he too had lived in Paris where he tended to socialise with James Stephens. 'In spite of sharp clashes and stormy disputes between the two men,' wrote Desmond Ryan, 'the link between them forged in the hardships and struggle of their Paris exile never really snapped. It is probable that Stephens regarded O'Mahony with greater affection than O'Mahony regarded him.'

In 1858 O'Mahony and Doheny persuaded Stephens to set about building an Irish Fenian organisation – the Fenians – which could coordinate its efforts with those of the American organisation. The Fenians, rejecting all activism other than armed struggle, were both the lineal descendents of the Young Irelanders and also an organisation which regarded that movement as being wrong-headed and amateur. They thought that the carry-on at Ballingarry – which they had witnessed with their own eyes and, ultimately, suffered the consequences of in imposed exile –had been humiliating, silly and disgraceful.

Fenians took an oath of allegiance to an Irish Republic, swearing to take up arms when called upon to do so by their revolutionary leaders. Stephens was given the job of preparing the groundwork in Ireland for a planned Fenian uprising.

When 1848 leader Terence Bellow McManus died in California in 1861 he was shipped back to Ireland for a hero's funeral. Michael Doheny was one of the Fenian luminaries who escorted the body on its long journey across America and the Atlantic to Dublin's Glasnevin Cemetery. According to legend, Doheny broke down and cried when he saw the coast of Ireland for the first time in thirteen years. He was greeted by sympathetic hordes at Cobh and, when he arrived at Limerick Junction *en route* to Dublin, the train line was blocked by cheering crowds who called out his name.

It seems certain that he undertook the journey home because he felt that the McManus funeral might provide a pretext or springboard for a rising. The more cautious Stephens, a great vacillator, orchestrated every aspect of the obsequies; he had no interest in any immediate revolution. After the funeral, and after being fobbed off by Stephens with good reasons why there could be no revolution just then, Doheny travelled south to Tipperary. On 28 November he entered Cashel in an open carriage, cheered on by huge crowds. The *Clonmel Herald* reported that the 'lower orders of the city' and 'hardy sons of toil' came out in force to welcome their returned hero. Banners across rooftops declared 'Cead mile Failte' and 'Eireann go bragh'. His warm reception in his adoptive home town was probably the high point of Doheny's political career and the only reward he got for a lifelong political commitment.

Doheny died from a fever in 1862 and, by the early 1860s, John O'Mahony was temporarily the undisputed leader of the Fenian Brotherhood in New York. The Brotherhood, despite having Irish-born leaders, came to perceive Irish separatism through the prisms of American ideology, American capital and American requirements. This set in train the vague and ultimately negative influence of right-wing American thinking upon Irish nationalist politics.

Over in Ireland Stephens travelled the land, disguised as a hobo, secretly recruiting Fenians. Kevin B. Nowlan has estimated that, by 1864-5, the Chief Organiser's efforts resulted in there being maybe 80,000 Fenians in Ireland and England, plus thousands of secret followers who were members of the British army.

Stephens was behind the foundation of a Dublin-based Fenian weekly newspaper, the *Irish People* in 1863. The ambitions which informed this venture were a desire to emulate the influence which *The Nation* had exerted over public opinion and the hope that the *Irish People* would raise badly-needed funds. Stephens felt that a conspiracy shouldn't publicise itself by putting out a paper, but he was convinced by others. His caution, in this regard, proved justifiable. It was their involvement with the *Irish People* which indirectly destroyed the lives of quite a few leading Fenians.

The first issue appeared on 28 November 1863. John O'Leary was editor-in-chief. O'Donovan Rossa, Thomas Clarke Luby and Charles J. Kickham were his editorial staff. It never made any real money, but it did successfully propagate the rebel Fenian agenda.

Once the paper was gone to the printers the team would usually retire to some tranquil surroundings to unwind and discuss the matters of the day. These gatherings tended to be frugal affairs, as befitted those living a revolutionary life, but for one such soiree a Cork supporter sent up a veritable banquet for the relaxing radicals. 'After the wild duck and snipe, which had come all the way from Cape Clear,' wrote Kickham, 'there came walnuts and oranges. It is fair to admit that there was also a decanter of what seemed to be the very best Irish whiskey, as Luby and O'Leary appreciated a stiff tumbler of whiskey punch … The "Chief Organiser" did not affect the more national beverage, but seemed to have a decided relish for a glass of Guinness' porter. Methinks I see him now – Shakespearian head, flowing auburn beard, lady hand, and all – as he takes his meerschaum from his lips, and pointing with the amber-tipped cherrywood tube to the table, says "If some people saw us now, what noise there would be about our luxurious habits!"'

A few weeks after the launch of the *Irish People*, O'Leary was left in complete charge when Stephens, despite the wild duck, the Guinness and the walnuts, withdrew from active day-to-day involvement.

John O'Leary was born into a Tipperary town merchant family in 1820 and educated there at the Abbey School before being sent to Carlow College. The journalist A.M. Sullivan said that he belonged, 'to one of the most worthy, amiable, and respectable families in Tipperary'. He studied law at Trinity College, Dublin, in 1847. It was at this time that he met up with like-minded activists such as Charles Gavan Duffy, Lalor and Meagher.

When he got out of prison after his involvement in the 1849 Wilderness affair, he briefly attended Cork University under the pretext of studying medicine. By 1855 he had drifted over to Paris where he socialised with bohemians such as the American painter Whistler before running into Stephens while visiting a boarding-house where his cousin lived. Despite Stephens' ardent promptings, O'Leary was pessimistic about the revolutionary possibilities provided by Ireland. He had inherited an income of several hundred pounds a year from his father and was quite content to potter around Paris buying and reading rare books. Someone who didn't much like O'Leary said that he was, 'reserved, sententious, almost cynical; keenly observant, sharply critical, full of restrained passion'.

When word got around Ireland that the *Irish People* was coming out, the paper's offices were inundated with that which all editors fear – unsolicited manuscripts. Sheaves of patriotic verse which appalled the exceptionally well-read O'Leary poured in. He said that, 'patriotism seems to take a peculiar delight in the manufacture of bad verse, while those who make a good article in this kind are too often not over patriotic'. In the twelfth issue of the paper he wrote: 'We have received this week such a pile of verses that, though very tired, we are tempted to give what we were going to call our poetical contributors a few hints. We confess we do this chiefly to save our own time; for though we are usually told that the authors are hard worked, and only write in the intervals of labour, we are afraid they must have too much time to spare, or rather to waste.'

The burden of editorship rested heavily on O'Leary's shoulders. Something of a literary snob, he felt that the 'talking and writing people' in Ireland were neither particularly rebellious nor much in favour of armed struggles. Ambitious about what he was doing, he put a great deal of his intellectual energies into finding semi-decent professional writers who might emulate the salon of bright and vivid prose stylists that *The Nation* had access to during its halcyon days. One of the few 'proper' writers that he could rely on was Charles J. Kickham.

Kickham was born at Mullinahone in 1828. His father was a wealthy storekeeper and Charles was related on his mother's side to John O'Mahony. When he was fourteen a shooting accident left him practically deaf and blind. He had organised the Mullinahone Confederate Club, playing minor roles in both the 1848 Rising and in the Tenant League. It fell to Kickham to fight, on behalf of the Fenians, a rhetorical war of attrition against their mortal foes, the Irish catholic church establishment.

What might be the feelings in a decent Christian's heart, Kickham once enquired in print, when he discovered that 'the dignitaries of his church, who know not want and nakedness themselves' were friendly with his oppressors? He wrote that, 'those who would prepare to grapple with the despoiler, and save a suffering people from destruction, are vilified and denounced' while at the same time, 'the place-beggar, the political mountebank, the ermined perjurer, the very exterminator – all these are courted and smiled upon and blessed'. Kickham said that he tended to agree with the Franciscan Luke Wadding who wrote: 'Time was when we had wooden chalices and golden priests, but now we have golden chalices and wooden priests.'

E.R.R. Green, in his essay *Charles Joseph Kickham and John O'Leary*, gives a delicately calibrated pen portrait of the two literary-minded Fenians: 'Charles Kickham and John O'Leary are the only literary figures produced by the Fenian movement who are at all deserving of the name, and even in their case there was no very striking achievement. O'Leary published one book, *Recollections of Fenians and Fenianism* (1896). which it must be admitted was well padded with material provided by his old comrade, Luby. Kickham's fame rests on a single novel, and although no book has enjoyed more popularity in Ireland, *Knocknagow* is by no means the greatest Irish work of fiction. Yet it must not be forgotten that these were men of action to whom the writing of books was not a primary concern. They were marked out by an identity of purpose, upheld with an integrity that typified the Fenian spirit to a younger generation … They had a good deal in common to start with; there was only about two years' difference between their ages and they were both Tipperary men of the same prosperous shop-keeping stock.'

Pierce Nagle, a traitor working in their midst at the *Irish People*'s offices, destroyed them. Nagle had been a teacher near Clonmel – Patrick C. Power says he had been a committed Fenian who was dismissed from his job because of his politics. He was, at any rate, recruited by the Irish Constabulary as a spy and provided them with a list containing the names of all the people who distributed the paper throughout the country and also the names of those who were in touch with the Fenian leadership.

According to Malcolm Brown, writing in *The Politics of Irish Literature*, Nagle 'felt his sensibilities bruised by Stephens' domineering manner. He sailed to New York and called on the British consulate officials to offer his services as a spy. A business arrangement was agreed upon, beginning with the payment of his fare back to Dublin, where he was hired by the *Irish People* as a wrapper in the mail room.'

In September 1865 he got his chance. A Clonmel Fenian visited the *Irish People*'s offices with a letter for Stephens, who gave the courier a typically hyperbolic message to take back to Tipperary: 'There is no time to be lost. This year must be the year of action. I speak with a knowledge and authority to which no other man could pretend, and I repeat the flag of Ireland – of the Irish Republic – must this year be raised.'

Stephens allegedly also gave the visitor some cash. As a result, later that same day, the Clonmel man returned to the offices in a drunken condition. Nagle seized the moment and, under the guise of taking care of the drunkard, got hold of Stephens' message to Tipperary. On 15 September detectives raided the *Irish People*'s offices, seized their files, and arrested everybody found there. Twenty three Fenians were arrested including O'Leary and, some time later, Kickham.

Many years later - according to legend - Nagle had the bad luck to bump into some old Fenians on a London street. He was severely beaten and died later as a result of his injuries.

Stephens' message didn't constitute proof that the paper's staff was engaged in a criminal conspiracy, so files and rubbish bins were trawled in the search for more solid evidence. Eventually an unpublished 'letter to the editor' was unearthed. In it the writer, regarded by O'Leary and the others as being half-cracked, said: 'The French exterminated their aristocracy, and every honest revolution must imitate that of France. We must do the same … the Irish aristocracy must be hounded down by the liberal press and slain afterwards by the hands of an aroused and infuriated people.'

A.M. Sullivan reported on O'Leary in the dock: 'His hair is dark, long, and thick, his moustache and beard are of the same colour, the latter flowing profusely over his breast, his prominent Roman nose and deep piercing eyes, set beneath fine eyebrows and a noble forehead, give an air of great command and determination to his countenance. And he not only seems, but is a gentleman, in mind, in manner, in education and in social position.'

As Kickham was led away to his cell, sentence having been passed on him, he noticed on the ground, and picked up, a picture of the Blessed Virgin. He piously kissed it and said to his warder: 'I have been accustomed to have the likeness of the Mother of God morning and evening before my eyes since I was a child. Will you ask the governor if I may keep this?'

O'Leary, Kickham and O'Donovan Rossa got long and cruelly enforced sentences. Rossa came out of prison a broken man; O'Leary and Kickham emerged into freedom, in their different ways, as damaged goods. O'Leary never liked to talk about his time in prison. Movingly, and with some dignity, he later said, 'I was in the hands of my enemy.'

Fragile Kickham's health collapsed during his incarceration. His abuse at the hands of his captors was raised in parliament in 1867. He was held in solitary confinement at Pentonville, subsequently transferred to Woking's hospital prison, and finally released in 1869. By then he was almost totally blind.

With the death of Michael Doheny and the jailing of O'Leary and Kickham, Tipperary Fenians ceased to have a day-to-day influence over the movement at a senior level. When risings eventually happened, in their absence, the Fenians enjoyed no more success than the much-maligned Young Irelanders.

An 1867 Rising was undermined by snowstorms which enveloped the country. At the same time, a traitor at the centre of the Fenian conspiracy, John Corydon, kept the authorities fully informed on their activities.

The commander in Tipperary was General Bourke, one of the numerous American Civil War veterans who'd flocked to the Fenian cause. Bourke, a native of Fethard whose family had emigrated to New York when their business collapsed during the Famine, took charge when General Godfrey Massey was arrested at Limerick Junction train station. Massey proved to be a real 'false traitor' and, to save his own skin, gave significant evidence against his comrades.

Bourke, flamboyant on horseback, led the Fenian forces at the Ballyhurst affray outside Tipperary town. Bourke's men were totally unprepared for action against disciplined British forces and the whole affair soon collapsed into disarray, with Bourke being arrested. A publican was ordered, after hours, to open up and to serve drink to thirsty Fenians. He was fired upon when he refused to do this. There were, however, significant barracks attacks at Ardagh and Kilmallock in Co. Limerick. Various police barracks were temporarily vacated a week after the Rising.

When the danger of revolt had passed, the British started mopping up small pockets of remaining Fenian resistance.

Tipperary was patrolled by troops organised into mobile anti-insurgent units called flying columns. The *Tipperary Free Press* reported that, 'gaols throughout the land have been glutted with the victims of a transatlantic swindle'.

Bourke was tried in Dublin and sentenced to death but, like other captured Fenians, his sentence was commuted. Kevin B. Nowlan wrote: 'A number of factors operated in favour of the prisoners. Bourke in particular impressed many by his bravery and obvious honesty of purpose and his trial was made all the more painful by the fact that his former colleague, Massey, gave evidence against him. It was also considered to their credit that the Fenians had committed no acts of violence against private property, and a final factor which may have disposed some towards leniency was the very small number of fatal casualties in the March Rising. An official police estimate, and it was probably reasonably accurate, put the total of fatal losses on both sides at about twelve … Cardinal Cullen, the archbishop of Dublin, despite his strong hostility to Fenianism, also intervened, making a personal plea to the authorities to commute Bourke's sentence.'

When O'Leary got out of prison he threw himself into political life and into life as the conscience of Fenianism. Whereas, awash with American sentimentalism, the movement gradually drifted off into intellectual shamrockery, nothing of that sort informed the severe, cerebral O'Leary.

He loathed the popular Fenian ballad 'God Save Ireland' and was affronted when, returning in triumph to Tipperary after years in jail and exile, his welcoming brass band played that tune. He once undertook an undercover Fenian fundraising trip to New York in discreet disguise. When he landed on the other side of the

Atlantic a brass band awaited him on the Battery pier and he was marched up Broadway, where a speech was demanded of him. 'The Irish-Americans overwhelmed him with picnics and oratory,' wrote Malcolm Brown 'and in Pittsburgh he listened to a sworn brother deliver as his own composition one of [Thomas Francis] Meagher's best-known oratorical war whoops. His American adventure forced him to disagree with the opinion of the poet Horace that men who cross seas change only their climate, not their dispositions.'

On a more serious level, it was O'Leary who sold the idea, central to Fenian thinking and to all Irish separatist thinking ever since, that there existed out in the mists of some semi-mythical Ireland a silent majority of people who, deep in their hearts, supported physical force or armed struggle against the British. It was from this notion or sense, rather than from any poll or election, that the IRA afterwards claimed their entire hypothetical mandate. 'It is the experience of what is now a pretty long life, with me,' wrote O'Leary, 'that the Fenian spirit is ever present in Ireland, and needs at any time but a little organisation to make it burst into renewed activity.' He stated that, 'The well-spring of nationality is in the heart of the people.' In 1896 he claimed that Fenianism had taught men, 'to sacrifice themselves for Ireland instead of selling themselves and Ireland to England'.

When Kickham was released from prison he devoted himself to writing and, despite his disabilities, enjoyed phenomenal success. His novel *Knocknagow* became one of the most popular of all Irish novels, and was still being widely read in the 1950s. One critic has pointed out that, while it wasn't a great achievement as a work of literature, it was a political and polemical novel which attacked that which it saw as being wrong, much like Marylyn

French's feminist novel, *The Women's Room* (1977) hit out on behalf of another political agenda in another age. *Knocknagow* attacked the landlord system in Ireland and, by implication, British rule which it perceived as underpinning that system. W.B. Yeats said that it was 'the most honest of Irish novels'.

In his occasional writings and in his fiction, Kickham identified himself as being a Tipperary man. He signed his articles and poems 'K. Mullinahone', 'C.J.K.', and 'Slievenamon'. His hugely popular ballads and poems included 'Rory of the Hill' and 'The Irish Peasant Girl', about the girl who 'lived beside the Anner at the foot of Slievenamon'. Popularly known as 'She Lived beside the Anner', this ballad is still part of the popular folk repertoire.

The Fenian movement was re-organised in the 1870s with a new constitution. Thereafter it was mainly known as the Irish Republican Brotherhood (IRB). Kickham headed the secret council that controlled it. He died in 1882.

On 27 November 1898, as part of the 1798* centenary celebrations, O'Leary returned to Tipperary town to unveil a statue of Kickham. People had travelled by train from all over Munster to attend the event. Those sharing the platform with O'Leary included the mayors of Cork and Clonmel. By then he was an elder statesman of dissent, befriended by a new generation of activists such as Arthur Griffith. W.B. Yeats, correctly described by T.W. Moody as O'Leary's most distinguished disciple, said that he was the 'handsomest old man' that he had ever seen, and that, 'from O'Leary's conversation and from the Irish books he lent or gave me, has come all I have set my mind to since'.

O'Leary was anxious that day in his home town to stress that, 'this statute is erected not in honour of the literary man ... but mainly … in honour of the patriot and politician'. He said that the time had now come to, 'lift the veil and tell an ignorant world that Charles Kickham had been the leader of the new Fenianism from his release from jail to the day of his death thirteen years later'.

John O'Leary died in 1907. The IRB, via Bulmer Hobson,* P.S. O'Hegarty,* and the Dungannon Clubs,* was by then reviving itself beyond all recognition so that it could play, at long last, the part in Irish history that its founders had dreamed of.

Yeats wrote that romantic Ireland was dead and gone, and with O'Leary in the grave. Nothing could have been further from the truth.

Seventy years after the events of 1848, Tipperary was about to lead again and, this time, Ireland was about to follow.

3

CONFUSION OR REVOLUTION?

During the last decades of the nineteenth century the IRB focused its considerable clandestine energies into entryism – overt and covert enrolment in Irish Ireland cultural bodies which enjoyed a great deal more popular support than the IRB's core code of armed resistance. Some of these organisations, such as the Gaelic Athletic Association (GAA), were partially the creation of the IRB. Others, such as the Gaelic League (which encouraged the revival of the Irish language), were initially non-political in their aspirations.

At a GAA meeting held in Thurles in September 1886 Patrick T. Hoctor, a left-wing IRB man, was elected vice-president of the association. A motion was willingly passed installing John O'Leary (by then the president of the IRB's Supreme Council) as a GAA Patron. At the same meeting the decision was taken to raise funds for the Tipperary town statue of Kickham and it was agreed that those who played ball games such as rugby or soccer would not be admitted into the GAA. This lurch towards a militant nationalist stance was partially orchestrated by Joseph K. Bracken, an old

Fenian stonemason whose sharp-witted son, Brendan Bracken, grew up to be Winston Churchill's wartime confidante and the founder of the *Financial Times*.

The IRB's structure in Tipperary had remained relatively strong during the decades of Parnellism* and the Land League.* With the nationwide revival of the movement in the early years of the twentieth century new Tipperary leaders, many of them Gaelic League-connected, emerged. These included Pierce McCan* from Dualla, Frank Drohan from Clonmel, Seamus O'Neill from Clonmel, Seán Treacy from Solohead, and Eamonn O'Duibhir from Ballagh. These men were, consecutively, a wealthy landowner, a prosperous Clonmel merchant, a teacher at the prestigious Rockwell College, a young farmer born to fourteen acres of land, and a prosperous farmer/entrepreneur.

The profession which stands out on this list is that of the farmer with the fourteen acres of land. Even in the Golden Vale of Tipperary, where all a farmer allegedly had to do was sit back and watch the cattle grazing, fourteen acres wasn't a huge stakehold in life.

All of the others conformed, in one way or the other, to a 'gentleman revolutionary' stereotype which harked back to both the Fenian and Young Irelander leadership. As the IRB's final and, in due course, most successful campaign got into full swing, various men of this sort withdrew from active involvement in the movement. Some moved over to the Sinn Féin side of things while others were sidelined by more militant elements.

McCan died in prison. Treacy was gunned down on the streets of Dublin.

The Fenian and Young Irelander rebellions may have floated

along on a wave of well meaning idealism but both movements lacked joined-up thinking and natural, decisive, leaders. In South Tipperary a significantly capable and thoughtful leadership cadre was about to emerge from within the group of young men who had Treacy at their core.

It was Treacy who recruited his childhood pal Dan Breen into the IRB. 'The IRB Circle to which we belonged was centered at Doon,' said Breen. 'There were very few people around our part of the country that could be relied upon and so we had to cycle eight or nine miles to attend those circle meetings. Packy Ryan of Doon was the Centre of the Circle and it was at Ryan's that I first met Seán McDermott* who, I believe, was on some kind of an organising mission around Munster. It may have been at Kilmallock because Packy Ryan also had a place there ... We were only ordinary members and, being little more than boys, we were just looked upon as handy messengers and suchlike, so we did not know about what was going on except what we could see for ourselves.'

When the IRB-backed 1916 Rising got under way in Dublin, it was groups of men under IRB command who, down in Tipperary, did their best to support the rebellion with armed resistance. The collective result of their efforts echoed the indecisiveness and confusion which had characterised both 1848 and 1867.

It was the sickening awareness of this which brought to the fore, post-1916, a generation of local leaders who took a more ruthless and radical approach to armed struggle. People like Treacy, Dan Breen, Dinny Lacey and Tommy Ryan were every bit as quick and political as the gentleman revolutionaries who'd initially been their leaders. They were sometimes a great deal more ideological than their well-heeled comrades. They were not, as Joost Augusteijn has unreasonably and patronisingly suggested, 'primarily attracted by the prospect of action'.

The Supreme Council of the IRB had resolved in January 1916 that the organisation would have an Easter Rising. Orders had gone out to all IRB Centres to prepare their Volunteers for involvement in the coming attempt to put an end to British rule in Ireland.

Clonmel's Volunteers trained and mobilised all through the spring of 1916, under the command of Frank Drohan. About fifty men, Drohan reckoned, were adequately prepared for the fight ahead. As was their wont, local IRB leaders played their cards close to their chests and told none of their foot soldiers exactly when this fighting might commence. Each of these Volunteers was reasonably well armed. Some had miniature BSA .22 rifles, some had Lee-Enfields, and a few had Smith and Wesson automatics.

The Rising was set in train on Holy Thursday 1916, when Patrick Pearse, believing that there was going to be an IRB-led revolt across the country, sent instructions to Liam Mellows* in Galway to activate Volunteer forces there.

'The goods will be delivered tomorrow night' was the coded message which signalled to the Clonmel republicans that the hour of battle was at hand. Willie Myles, a reporter at the Clonmel *Nationalist*, was given that message, under Clonmel's West Gate, on Holy Saturday 1916. 'At the time,' Myles remembered, 'I was returning to work at the *Nationalist* office, after dinner … I went on to an evening of suppressed excitement and tension. I was imagining to myself what a shock my fellow workers and the people in general would get the following night, or rather on the Monday, when they became aware of the history-making events that were about to break upon them.'

Frank Drohan's coachbuilder's yard was converted into a munitions factory and frantic last minute preparations were carried out. Volunteers worked night and day on the filling of cartridges and the preparation of explosives. The Clonmel conspirators were particularly fortunate because Myles, from his pew at the *Nationalist*, was privy to all manner of useful information which inevitably flowed into the paper's newsroom.

In Clonmel's 1916 commemorative publication *Cluain Meala* Myles' input was clarified: 'He was able to ascertain exact details of troop movements, actual strength of British forces in the various local barracks, and other relevant information censored by the British authorities. Late on Good Friday night, he arrived with information about the arrest in Kerry of Roger Casement,* and the death of Donal Sheehan* at Ballycissane Pier, Killorglin. The impact on those present at Drohan's house – Seamus O'Neill, Bob Drohan, and Tom Halpin – was one of shock and fear that the plans for the impending rebellion might now be known to the authorities.'

On Saturday morning Eamonn O'Duibhir sent a telegram to Seamus O'Neill in Clonmel while Con Deere of Goold's Cross showed up in the town. They both had news that the expected Rising was due to kick off in Dublin the following afternoon, Easter Sunday. The Dublin rebellion was to be accompanied by armed revolution in every provincial district.

'On Easter Sunday morning,' Frank Drohan said, 'I had all the officers in our yard, the coach building yard in Irishtown, arranging what we were going to do. I sent a messenger named John Mackey over to Fethard. The orders I had got to rise gave no details as to what precisely we were to do. This was left entirely to ourselves.

There were no other Volunteer units surrounding us, although we had IRB Circles in places like Fethard and Cashel. The Clonmel Volunteer Company was more or less isolated. Pierce McCan had a little crowd of Volunteers up at Dualla and he had gone up to Dublin when he got the news on Saturday to make sure that everything was alright because Pierce was a very careful man. Knowing he had gone up, I sent Seamus O'Neill across to meet him when he came back. Seán Treacy from Tipperary also went to meet him.'

O'Neill headed for Goold's Cross to await McCan's return. On his way to his rendezvous he stopped off at Fethard to tell the local leader, Paddy Henehan, to be ready for action.

In a house near Cashel O'Neill anxiously awaited McCan in the company of Seán Treacy, Eamonn O'Duibhir, Michael Sheehan of Dundrum and others. O'Duibhir was told to meet McCan at the train station as it was felt that a crowd of known militants would arouse suspicion. McCan gave O'Duibhir a message for the assembled Volunteer leaders: 'The rising is on, starting in Dublin at 4 p.m. tomorrow (Sunday). The Pope has sent his blessing through Count Plunkett. The Germans are to launch a big air-raid on England, to cover the landing of German officers, arms and ammunition in Ireland.'

'Our next meeting will be in an Irish Republic.' Treacy is said to have declared as these leaders prepared to go back to their respective districts with the news.

O'Neill returned to Clonmel where, straight away, he brought the message to Drohan's house. An order to mobilise at 10 a.m. on Sunday morning was issued, and conveyed by word of mouth to most of the local Volunteers.

'The strategy which had been decided upon was simple,' says *Cluain Meala*. 'The British had large forces in Clonmel, Cahir and Fethard; to attack these barracks would have been lunacy, and so it was decided to march to Lisronagh [a village between Clonmel and Fethard], join up with the Fethard Volunteers and attack the RIC barracks at Lisronagh.'

'I sent John Mackey over to Fethard on the Sunday morning,' said Frank Drohan, 'to tell the Fethard fellows, the few of them that were there, to come into Lisronagh and that we would meet them there and capture Lisronagh RIC Barracks. After that we would attack places like Clerihan and such outlying barracks where there were only five or six police as we felt unable to deal with anything in Clonmel itself where, in addition to a strong barracks of twenty or more police, there was also a military barracks. We aimed to move on towards Cashel then and link up there with Pierce McCan where we hoped to be able to take Cashel barracks that night.

'While we were going over these plans, John Mackey returned and with him were two men in a motor car. They were waiting for me outside the yard. These men were the bearers of a message informing me that the whole thing had been called off, that is, that the rising would not take place as planned … This news startled me and my heart sank. I felt that this was a repetition of the Fenian Rising, that somebody had given away the game or something like that.'

Willie Myles, along with section commander Michael White, was present in Drohan's yard when they heard about the cancellation. 'About 10.30 a.m. or so White and myself were in the coach painting shop at the back of Frank Drohan's house taking some rifles out of their hiding place. We were starting to clean and oil them when P.J. Henehan and Seán O'Shea of Fethard arrived by car with a message for Frank Drohan who was with White and myself. The message was from McCan and was to the effect that the order for the Rising had been countermanded by Eoin Mac Neill, then President of the Volunteers, and as far as most of the Volunteers in the provinces were concerned, the most important man in the organisation … White and myself put the rifles back into hiding believing that the affair had been a test or trial of some kind. In the afternoon we went to Grangemockler to play in a football championship against Mullinahone. The Volunteer members of the team had been told the previous night to turn out with the team so as not to arouse any suspicion.'

The O'Rahilly* had travelled south from Dublin by car with the countermanding order. Pierce McCan was sent on to Limerick with the new instructions and these were then passed on to Killarney. The O'Rahilly drove to Cork while Drohan headed off towards Waterford and New Ross with the news.

The confusion which characterised Volunteer efforts in Clonmel was also to be found in the Tipperary town area. 'When I came home for Easter,' Dan Breen said, 'Seán Treacy told me he expected a rising to take place on Easter Sunday, but when the cancellation messages were received he told me about them and I went back to my work beyond Kilmallock … Having heard further messages of the rising in Dublin I returned home again on Tuesday until the Friday of that week … he [Treacy] was away from home and, so we learned since, was cycling around from one centre to another trying to urge the Tipperary Volunteers to take action to support the fighting in Dublin.'

On Easter Monday Frank Drohan was back in Clonmel, exhausted and disheartened, having delivered the countermanding orders to the South East. 'On Easter Monday,' said Myles, 'we had no word of the rising in Dublin up to the time. I left Clonmel for Mount Melleray (about 3 p.m.). The following day was prize-distribution day there and my job was to report the proceedings for the *Nationalist*. On Tuesday morning, in Mount Melleray, the *Cork Examiner* photographer had the exciting news for the good monks and all of us that a boat believed to be carrying arms had been sunk off the south coast. About 2 p.m. there were rumours going around that the "Sinn Féiners" were out in Dublin and that Dublin Castle had been taken.'

Rumours of war were beginning to seep into Clonmel too. 'On Easter Monday evening,' said Drohan, 'there was a circus passing through the town and I was standing at the door watching it when Tom Halpin ... came along. He was at that time a clerk in the railway. He said to me that the Volunteers must not have all got word of the cancellation of the arrangements as some engineer or someone who had come up in a train had told him that the railway was torn up at Rathdowney or somewhere like that. We felt rather sorry for these fellows not having got word and having gone out on their own when nobody else was out. That night some people who came back from Dublin told us that there was fighting in Dublin, shooting all over the place, but we could get no definite information as to what was going on. We had stopped all our fellows from going to Dublin that day, to the Fairyhouse races, but one man who was not a Volunteer but the brother of a Volunteer had gone up to the races and had not returned. He could not get back.'

When Myles returned from reporting on the prize giving at Mount Mellary's boarding school he had with him a message that, 'There is fighting in Dublin – believed to be the Citizen Army*; no exact details as to the course of the fighting.' Drohan now sent out more orders to his Volunteers telling them, 'to hold themselves ready for a call-out'. Known IRB men in Clonmel decided to go into hiding. A new IRB headquarters was established at sawmills on the Dungarvan Road.

Late on Monday evening, rumours reached Tipperary town which suggested that there was something happening in Dublin. A small group of Volunteers watched the roads around the home of the IRB boss in that part of the county, Eamonn O'Duibhir. Soon they were joined by Seán Treacy, travelling by bike. He slept at O'Duibhir's that night and the following day he cycled on to various Tipperary districts searching of information.

On Monday night a Volunteer meeting took place in Treacy's absence at the Workmen's Club in Tipperary town. Those present included Dinny Lacey, later to enjoy fame as a member of the Third Tipperary Brigade and as the leader of a South Tipperary flying column, and Mick O'Callaghan, a founding member of the Workingmen's Protection and Benefit Society. O'Callaghan, a local firebrand in favour of immediate action was, at the time of the Easter Rising, manager of the Condensed Milk Company's Lattin creamery. Others present at the Workmen's Club meeting made the point that, since it was impossible to get any accurate news from Dublin, there was little point in the Tipperary Volunteers showing their hand just then. Treacy was known to be in favour of combat.

The meeting was adjourned until the next evening, Tuesday, when the Volunteers met up yet again. This assembly proved to be equally inconclusive. Afterwards a frustrated Mick O'Callaghan was heading for home when he ran into a large crowd of pro-British citizenry. Their politics was usually attributed by nationalists to their connection with the British army, who had a large barracks in the town. It seems that there were sizeable pockets of loyalist catholics in towns like Tipperary and Cahir.

The hostile crowd singled O'Callaghan out for verbal abuse, mobbed him, and started hurling stones at him. RIC men, observing the scuffle, refused to intervene. O'Callaghan took refuge in a house but his attackers began to break down the house's front door. O'Callaghan threatened to shoot in order to defend himself. Then the police intervened and called on him to surrender. He refused to do this.

When the RIC started kicking in the door O'Callaghan *did* open fire with his Colt automatic and the police temporarily withdrew. The house was kept under surveillance but O'Callaghan managed to escape by a rear entrance. He made his way into mountains six miles from Tipperary where he hid in the home of his cousin.

When he was resting there the following afternoon, a Sergeant O'Rourke and a Constable Hurley walked into the house. O'Rourke, who knew O'Callaghan well, placed his hand on his shoulder as if to arrest him, at the same time asking him his name and line of business.

"Here's my card!" said O'Callaghan, grabbing for his revolver and shooting O'Rourke dead on the spot. Constable Hurley rushed out of the house, but O'Callaghan shot him down just as he reached the door. These men were the only 1916 fatalities outside of Dublin.

O'Callaghan soon afterwards took the traditional Fenian route into exile, escaping to New York via Liverpool.

Dan Breen said that Seán Treacy considered that the good name of Tipperary had been saved during Easter week by O'Callaghan who, he wrote in *My fight For Irish Freedom*, 'escaped to the United States of America, and the following year was arrested by Federal agents and held prisoner in the notorious Tombs prison of New York. Extradition proceedings were instituted against him. Treacy and I made up our minds that if he was brought back for trial in Ireland, we would do our utmost to rescue him.'

On the Tuesday Eamonn O'Brien, leader of the Galtee battalion was approached on the main street in Galbally by a stranger, a bespectacled cyclist who turned out to be Seán Treacy. Treacy told O'Brien that all Volunteers were to rise up. Before he cycled on, Treacy supervised preparations for a raid on the post office where some four thousand rounds of shotgun ammunition were captured. He told the locals to block the roads and to cut all lines of communication.

Moving on to Ballylanders, Treacy suggested that Anglesboro barracks should be hit. At this stage he heard about the countermanding orders which had been sent down from Dublin. These didn't seem, in any way, to temper his hunger for action. He cycled on towards Cork city. At Mitchelstown he ran into a car coming from Cork flying a white flag, and heard that the rebellion in the south had entirely failed. The car contained Volunteers who told Treacy that Cork's Volunteer Hall was surrounded by British heavy guns and that a truce had been declared.

On Thursday, when they hooked up at Packy Ryan's hotel in Doon, Treacy filled O'Duibhir in on what he had discovered during his travels. Ryan, one of the leading IRB lights in Munster, was the man who'd hosted the gathering at which Dan Breen had met Seán McDermott. As Treacy, O'Duibhir and Ryan discussed the situation far away from the action, McDermott was, with the other 1916 leaders, fighting the fight of his life in Dublin's GPO.

Ryan advised the others that the situation in Limerick and Tipperary was hopeless. It was decided that Ryan would return to his home while Treacy and O'Duibhir would attempt to reach Dublin in order to throw their lot in with the GPO rebels.

O'Duibhir was arrested in Killenaule by RIC men. Treacy made several attempts to reach Dublin but could not travel by train or, given the general disruption, by road. He thought about linking up with Liam Mellows over in Galway but nothing came of this notion. Myth has it that he cycled as far as the Shannon before gloomily turning back towards Doon.

'There is no doubt whatever,' wrote Desmond Ryan in *Seán Treacy and the Third Tipperary Brigade*, 'that of all the Tipperary Volunteer leaders Seán Treacy, at the time ranked as a First Lieutenant, was a man with a stronger influence than this rank might suggest. Treacy was the man who made the most determined effort to set the county ablaze. His endurance as a long distance cyclist both then and later, when work was afoot, astonished his comrades.'

Back in Clonmel, confusion still reigned. As Desmond Ryan put it, their situation was 'bewildering and obscure'. Military censorship was in effect so the only news that local leaders got was rumour and gossip. Drohan sent a message to McCan that the Clonmel Volunteers were ready to fight. McCan in turn sent out messages to Cork and to Limerick, stating that South Tipperary would rise up immediately if Cork and Limerick did so.

By Wednesday the Clonmel Volunteers were hugely frustrated but still gung ho; they decided, as their predecessors had unwisely decided in past times, that they would come out in open rebellion whatever the consequences. They heard that the fighting in Dublin was still going on and that the British had brought in heavy artillery.

'On Wednesday night,' said Drohan, 'the news appeared in the local paper here, the *Nationalist*, that the fighting was all over in Dublin and that everything was quiet. It was not "the Rising" the paper said, but "the fighting". I afterwards learned that it was the District Inspector of the RIC in Clonmel who had put in this notice and of course the *Nationalist* had to publish it.'

On Thursday morning McCan sent out a message to the effect that 'Cork and Kerry are out. Limerick is coming out.' Drohan issued orders that all the Clonmel Volunteers were to assemble at Rathronan Cross – a couple of miles to the west of Clonmel – at 1pm, bringing all of their weapons, ammunition and equipment with them. Headquarters staff returned to Drohan's yard. A message was sent out to Fethard: the plan to attack Lisronagh barracks, decided upon earlier in the week, was to be activated.

Approximately twelve armed Volunteers gathered at Rathronan Cross at the designated time, with others taking up positions in the surrounding fields, but Frank Drohan never showed up. A messenger arrived with instructions to the effect that the planned attack was cancelled. This resulted in a heated argument and the messenger was sent back into town to seek written confirmation. Drohan's brother brought the requested verification within half an hour. The men were dismissed and ordered to return to their homes through the fields and by boreens.

Apparently Eamonn O'Duibhir had gone to Limerick and found no fighting going on there. Pierce McCan sent a message containing this news to Drohan, who decided to immediately go see McCan and seek clarity. They agreed to postpone the Lisronagh strategy until they got definite word concerning the situation in Cork and Kerry.

Those IRB/Volunteer leaders were fully aware that some serious fighting was going on in Dublin. They had been instructed to make their own plans in Tipperary. They could have taken positive revolutionary action, irrespective of the situation in the neighbouring counties. The Fenians, the Young Irelanders, the GPO rebels, and the people clustered around Seán Treacy over in Tipperary town, had all been reckless or impetuous spirits. In Clonmel, caution was their watchword.

Frank Drohan enjoyed a lifelong reputation for decency and sincerity but history has also bestowed on him a reputation for being overly hesitant and indecisive. Reading between the lines, one gets the sense that he was too nice a man for the rough and tumble of actual revolution. His pal Willie Myles said that he was, 'beyond all doubt the father of the Volunteers in Clonmel. Too gentle and kindly perhaps to make a ruthless man of action, he would have accepted any suffering for the cause of liberty.' The *Nationalist* later called him, 'one of Tipperary's most esteemed public men'. Michael Ahearn, in his recent magisterial study of Clonmel personalities, says: 'Frank Drohan's patriotism was expressed in other ways. Even in the very early years when Irish-manufactured articles were not comparable in standard to imported ones, Frank Drohan would purchase only Irish made goods. When, on his withdrawal from politics, he settled down to running his late wife's grocery shop at 16 Upper Irishtown, he continued to promote the sale of Irish products. Not forgetting his love for the Irish language, he encouraged his customers, especially the school children, to whom he was affectionately known as "the Irishman", to converse in Irish.'

In 1909 or 1910, working his way through Gaelic League branches, it was Drohan who'd established an IRB Circle in Clonmel and who'd later been active in the formation of Circles in Ballagh, Cashel, Fethard, Thurles and Tipperary.

On Friday morning a scout was sent by motorbike to Cork to find out exactly what was going on. His mission was to contact Terence MacSwiney or Thomas MacCurtain, the leading Cork Volunteers. He managed to track down McCurtain and returned to Clonmel with the news that 'Cork is not rising, but if there is any change a lady will come by train to Clonmel to inform you'.

Late on Friday night Willie Myles brought word that the British were closing in on rebel positions in Dublin and that the centre of the city was burning. On Saturday morning, Myles reported that there were rumours of surrender. That afternoon, a notice was posted in the main post office in Clonmel that the 'rebels have surrendered'. This couldn't be confirmed until uncensored Sunday papers arrived in town. Frank Drohan then issued orders that all arms, ammunition and equipment was to be hidden, and that nothing should be surrendered to the authorities.

Seán Horan, who played a significant part in the approaching war as a member of the Third Tipperary Brigade, was terribly demoralised by the failure of the Rising when he ran into Treacy in Tipperary town. 'I felt a bit unhappy until I met Seán,' Horan said. 'In Easter Week 1916, I left my work with the intention of getting to Dublin to assist my fellow countrymen there. In the town of Tipperary on Easter Monday night, I got to know there was no chance of getting into the city of Dublin so I returned home. Seán got to know my mind; it was through Dan Breen that I met him. Seán questioned me and asked me if I belonged to any other armies or Volunteer forces. I told him that I was in the National Volunteers since they started, in order to be trained to fight against England for the freedom of Ireland, and not for sport. Before Seán and I parted that evening he invited me to Lisheen Grove, two and a half miles from Tipperary town. He gave instructions about the collecting of arms, and asked who in the company had any. I said I had a double-barreled shotgun, and Seán said that was very good. The company was then small, about ten men, and later it numbered fifteen … Seán Treacy was very cautious as to whom he would invite into the company in Lisheen Grove after the Rising, whilst training was going on secretly. That kept the company small … Seán Treacy was a very far-seeing man. He saw years ahead of him. He also had the gift of gaining everyone's favour. The Lisheen Grove officers decided to go to the outside parishes and get companies working. So Seán Treacy went to Mount Bruis. Dan Breen and I went to Solohead and Cappawhite. We paraded each company, and when we had finished, we went to Mount Bruis. When we met with Seán he was drilling about twenty ladies! I remarked to Seán: "What will you put the ladies to doing, Seán?"

"'Well," said he, "they'll be put to something. They can carry despatches."

'He had a company of men there also.'

'Hitherto we had looked to the townspeople as being more in touch with things,' said Dan Breen, 'and perhaps as countrymen we suffered some sense of inferiority. Now however, for some reason, after the rising the townspeople were more inclined to look to us and so conditions were reversed. Treacy and I went about to all the towns like Tipperary, Cahir, and other places about there and urged the reorganisation of the Volunteers.'

The RIC reported that: 'A discontented and rebellious spirit is widespread, and though to a great extent suppressed, it frequently comes to the surface at Gaelic Athletic Association tournaments when large numbers of young men of military age are assembled together. On such occasions the Irish Republican badge is conspicuously worn, and seditious songs and cries of "Up the Rebels", "To Hell with England", etc. are indulged in.'

'One day,' said Seán Horan, 'Seán was writing at a table there alone. I just remarked to him: "Do you think, Seán, the fight will soon be over? I am deaf, stupid and blind from travelling and working for Irish freedom." Seán took off his glasses and said, "Jack, the fight could last a hundred years, one hundred years!"'

4

TIPPERARY, 1917

In the immediate aftermath of the 1916 Rising a substantial cross-section of the Volunteer/IRB elite was arrested and imprisoned. Many of these ended up in far-away prisons like Wales' Frongoch camp or Reading Jail near London. In Ireland there was a backlash against the execution of the 1916 leaders. Those who survived to be locked up in British jails, initially perceived as troublemakers, were now looked upon as heroes in certain nationalist circles.

By Christmas 1916 events were moving ahead briskly on all fronts; they moved ahead with dynamic speed until the end of the Civil War six years later. Aware that they had made martyrs out of the 1916 ringleaders, the British started releasing the remaining leaders and activists. A cadre of hardened and intellectually honed militants came back into Irish society emboldened by their burgeoning popularity and inspired by the perceived martyrdom of Pearse, Connolly, *et al*.

The IRB wanted to cash in on the waves of sympathy which greeted the returning prisoners. They deliberately sent out to the provinces capable organisers who could assist local leaders in the training of fighters. The lessons of the past had finally been learned and the militant separatist movement was determined to put itself on a proper war footing.

At the same time drifting radicals, vaguely in hiding or vaguely on the run, washed up in parts of Ireland previously unfamiliar to them. The lives of militants, imprisoned and otherwise, had been profoundly disrupted in the aftermath of the Rising. The country was in a pre-revolutionary flux.

Political visitors to Tipperary early in 1917 included two Westmeath brothers, Tom and Seamus Malone, a republican priest called Fr Feeney, Belfast-born 1916 leader Seamus Robinson, and a Galway school teacher, Brigid Walsh, who'd also played an active role in the Rising.

Eamonn O'Duibhir, in Reading Jail, got to know Seamus Robinson, who had played an intrepid role in the Dublin Rising. O'Duibhir noted Robinson's obvious sincerity and capability. After their release he invited the firm catholic to come live at his Kilshenane farm as an alleged farm labourer. In fact Robinson's job was to help manage the Volunteers.

'Robinson arrived some day in January 1917,' said O'Duibhir, 'in the midst of a snow storm, and he had with him a small black travelling bag that we got to know very well and to associate with him. As a farm worker he made up for his lack of knowledge by his honesty, hustle, and zeal. He certainly worked as hard as he could and left nothing undone that he could do, and in addition to all that he was a very gentlemanly man.'

Tom Malone had previously lived in Donohill, near Tipperary town, as a Gaelic League teacher. In that context he had become friendly with local men like Seán Treacy and Dan Breen. He now re-established contact with Treacy and Breen, and got to know the recently arrived Robinson. Tom had just been elected to the Volunteer Army Council with IRB support. He was sent, early in 1917, to west Limerick – a GHQ man – to knock the local Volunteers into shape. Padraic O'Farrell describes Tom Malone as being 'an astoundingly successful leader'. Aware that the South Tipperary Volunteers were better organised and motivated than most other units, he took an interest in what they were up to and kept a watching brief on them.

'They were a grand collection of men,' said Tom. 'Eamonn O'Duibhir of Ballagh, Dan Breen, Ned O'Reilly, Seamus Robinson, Paddy Kinnane, Jimmy Leahy, Joe McLoughlin and Micksey Connell of Thurles, most of them to become well known in the fight afterwards … We planned to ambush and disarm four RIC guarding a boycotted farm. That was two years before Soloheadbeg. We lay in wait, O'Dwyer, Kinnane, Breen, Treacy, and myself, but they did not come at the right time. We raided Molloy's of Thurles and carried away eight boxes of gelignite.'

Tom Malone's brother, Seamus Malone, was theoretically an Irish teacher in Tipperary in 1917 who nurtured the cultural and social changes which went hand in hand with the emergent militancy. He too, having been released from prison, travelled south to do IRB organising work.

'I had a letter from Seán Hurley asking me to go to County Limerick as a travelling Irish teacher and as a representative of the Brotherhood.' said Seamus. 'I had another from Ned O'Dwyer, whom I had met in prison, asking me to take up a similar post in Tipperary … I decided to go to Tipperary … I arrived at Drumbane, in the centre of County Tipperary, at the end of January 1917. That first night I met Brigid Walsh who was Secretary to the Regional

Council of the Gaelic League. Brigid was a schoolteacher in Drumbane ... Although I had never before met her I knew her by reputation from Liam Mellows for a couple of years.'

Seamus married Brigid Walsh who, at the time of the Rising, had travelled from Dublin to Galway with military instructions for Mellows. 'When the Volunteers were dispersed she brought Fr Feeney, who was their chaplain, back with her to Tipperary,' said Malone. 'The priest was on the run and was being hotly pursued, but she kept him concealed until Sir John Maxwell* decided to leave him for correction to the Bishop of Galway. Fr Feeney said that Maxwell, at his worst, could not have been half as hard on him as was the bishop. It was Brigid likewise who had gone to Cork to arrange the passage to America for Liam Mellows and his comrades. An old sailor in Cork, a Captain Collins, assisted her in the job.'

Paddy Kinnane, later involved in attacks on Holycross and Rearcross barracks, confirmed Seamus Malone's version of events: 'Soon after the Rising Seán Broderick of Galway, accompanied by a priest (whose name was I think Fr\ Feeney) came to our neighbourhood. They were both on the run, and they stayed at Stapleton's of Finnahy. The reason they came to our district was that Broderick was acquainted with a Galway lady, a Miss Walsh, who later became Mrs Seamus Malone and was then a teacher in Drumbane.'

There were, at that time, six branches of the Gaelic League under the control of Brigid Walsh's Drumbane Regional Committee. These branches were in Drumbane, Ballagh, Rossmore, Upperchurch, the Ragg and Inch. 'They were all within five miles of me, except Inch, which was a couple of miles further on,' said

Seamus Malone. 'I spent one night per week in each place. There was an Irish class from eight to nine-thirty, a *ceili* from nine-thirty to eleven-thirty, and I drilled the Volunteers for an hour after that. There were classes for the schoolchildren in the evenings. I spent the day travelling the countryside, trying to set up new branches or representing the Volunteers or the Brotherhood. Some branches held a big *ceili* every Sunday night, as a rule, and in the fine weather there was a *feis* somewhere on the Sunday. We went on bicycles to the *feises* and to the ceilis. Well known speakers from Dublin and from other places attended the *feises* for the purpose of exhorting the people. If there were no *feis* in our vicinity we went to a football or hurling match and held a public meeting there. I can assure you that we were seldom idle. The travelling teacher usually had a salary of a hundred pounds, but he had often to collect the money himself.'

Malone was brought before the courts when a poem he recited at a political-cultural event held alongside the Rock of Cashel was deemed subversive. At court he was fined £1, which he refused to pay. Every day after that he expected the police to come looking for him but somebody paid his fine unbeknownst to him.

Paddy Kinnane was sworn into the IRB by Eamonn O'Duibhir, and was given permission to swear in recruits. He proceeded to do this in outlying districts, but did so with some caution.

'The next move took place in February 1917,' said Kinnane, 'when a branch of the Gaelic League was formed in Upperchurch. The prime mover behind the formation of the branch was also Eamon O'Duibhir. Seamus Malone and his brother Tom came to Upperchurch as Irish teachers, and classes were also held in Rossmore, Drumbane, the Ragg and Ballagh. Soon afterwards

Sinn Féin clubs were formed in the same areas. Some months later a company of Irish Volunteers was organised which became known as the Upperchurch company, or the Upperchurch Volunteers. The nucleus of a company was there through the men who had been sworn into the IRB and through the Gaelic League branch and the Sinn Féin club. I was the first captain of this company; the other officers were James Larkin and the late James Stapleton. The strength of the company was about thirty five or forty men. No arms were than available, but we held regular parades and practiced foot drill.'

The Malone brothers soon found that their Irish language classes and their IRB reorganisation work was bringing them to the attention of the local police. Tom Malone was arrested and jailed along with Seamus O'Neill, the Clonmel IRB leader. Seamus Malone decided it would be prudent to go on the run before he was jailed again: 'We held the classes secretly and we always had guards posted. The secret work suited the people very well. Many houses were searched for me but, although it was often a near thing, I somehow always managed to escape. There were a great number of police and soldiers in Drumbane. It was the first place in Ireland in which the military assisted the police. There was some land agitation taking place but the Volunteers were not involved in it. One farmer was boycotted and a crowd of policemen were guarding him. I often slept in this man's house while the police were outside. I was quite safe in the very midst of the enemy. When the chase became too hard I was compelled to give up teaching the classes. Brigid Walsh did the work for me for a spell before the summer holidays. That gave me more time for the work of the Volunteers and the Brotherhood.'

Malone found out a great deal about rural life in Tipperary during his time of outlaw subsistence. On one occasion he was hiding out in the hills with trigger happy RIC men hot on his heels. 'I found a mountain cabin and went in to look for something to eat,' he recalled. 'I was starved with the hunger. There were two brothers and two sisters in the house. They were all over sixty and they each weighed at least twenty stone. They were gentle, generous people. They had heard the shots and knew what was happening. They had a great welcome for me. They invited me to stay the night with them and take my ease. I only needed the word.

'Bed time came. Myself and the two old men went into a room. There were two big comfortable beds there. They were so big that it was almost impossible to walk between the beds and the wall. I went into one bed. One of the men jumped into the bed after me and the other jumped in after him. When all was quiet the door opened. A woman stuck in her head …

'"Is he asleep, Mike?" said she. I pretended to be.

'The man nearest to me listened …

'"He is," said he.

'Then the two women came in in their long night-gowns and went into the other bed and we all five of us slept soundly until morning. And when I rose I noticed that there were only the two rooms in the house. Although the house was narrow it was scoured clean and everything was in proper order. I received an invitation to come again and I did. The house was in a very out-of-the-way place and it was very difficult to find for one who didn't know the lie of the land. The police never came as long as I was in the district.'

Seán Treacy began to emerge as a determined Volunteer leader. The old leadership had, to some extent, lost authority and influence due to their inability to come out fighting during the Rising. Treacy, by way of contrast, had been spoiling for a fight.

In Tipperary town a new branch of the Gaelic League was set up – Craobh Phadraic Mhic Phiarais (Patrick Pearse Branch) – with Treacy as president and his friend Dinny Lacey as secretary. Advanced Irish classes were taken by 'Professor' Sam Fahy, purportedly one of the authors of Dan Breen's *My Fight for Irish Freedom*. A Volunteer Hall was founded at Eaton's Cottages and Sinn Féin extended its influence in the town, meetings being held at the Labour Hall. Treacy, Lacey and Breen had some involvement in Sinn Féin politics but by March 1917 they were principally concerned with Volunteer work, forming or reorganising companies.

Tadgh Crowe was one of the men recruited by Treacy. 'In the early months of 1917,' Crowe said, 'the late Seán Treacy asked me to become a member of the Irish Volunteers. I agreed and, at his request, I got two others in the parish, my cousin Joe McCormack, and Tom Ryan, to join. From three we built our strength up to eight and Seán Treacy came along on one or two nights each week and drilled and trained us at an old fort in a grove near Limerick Junction. That was the beginning of what later became E/Company, Fourth Battalion, Third Tipperary Brigade.

'Secrecy was then the golden rule in all matters relating to the Volunteers. Quietly we built up the strength to twenty and later to sixty-three. Seán Treacy conducted an election of company officers at which both he and I were proposed for company captain. Seán was then recognised as Volunteer organiser and leader in South Tipperary, but he was a man who would never seek rank. He allowed his name to go forward simply because it was the correct thing to do and to comply with the general rule of the members' right to elect their own officers. For the purpose of the record I will mention that I beat him by three votes, thirty three to thirty.'

'Some time about April 1917 Seán Treacy made a few trips to the locality and suggested the organising of a Volunteer unit there,' said Tommy Ryan from Ballylooby, a future Vice Commandant of the Third Tipperary Brigade, 'On his second visit to us, he gave us an outline of the organisation and generally encouraged us, pointing out what should be done and how to do it. As a result of Treacy's visit, the Battalion was formed with Ned McGrath as the Battalion Commandant. I was Vice Commandant. This was really the beginning of my career in the Volunteer movement. Following Treacy's instructions, we set to work from then on to organise Companies in the surrounding parishes, to appoint officers for these, and to direct their training.'

The organising of companies was difficult, said Ryan, 'because the European war was not yet over and the general sympathies of the people around were still tending towards the British. In villages where, in the Redmondite* Volunteer days, they were able to raise Companies of one hundred to one hundred and fifty, we were only able to get together five or six or ten at the outside … The Battalion area extended from Newcastle, Co. Tipperary, to the borders of Mitchelstown, along by the Galtees into Cahir. That was the Sixth Battalion area of the South Tipperary Brigade. In the political sphere the people around were generally supporters of the Irish Party. There was, therefore, no one to undertake political propaganda for the electioneering work except the Volunteers. The responsibility for this branch of activity became a primary duty of the Battalion Staff.'

Paddy 'Lacken' Ryan, immortalised in Ernie O'Malley's hugely literate IRA memoirs, remembered the early days of Volunteer organising: 'On a night in the early summer of 1917 I attended a meeting which was held in a place called Downey's Barn at Cramp's Castle, Fethard. This meeting was called for the purpose of organising an Irish Volunteer company in Fethard and district … The meeting itself was a small one, as for obvious reasons only a selected number of men were invited to attend. I should say, however, that there were about twenty men present, all of whom agreed to become members of the Volunteer organisation.'

Through Treacy's influence seven companies had been formed by the summer of 1917, each company fifty to sixty strong. Secret drilling began in earnest.

Paddy O'Dwyer of Hollyford was another of Treacy's inner circle. Once he and Treacy, being hungry, called around to a neighbour's house. There was nobody home and the doors and windows of the house were well fastened. Treacy knew that, some time before, a bullet fired during practice had left a small hole above the fastener of one of the windows. He asked Dwyer for a piece of wire.

'Seán and Paddy,' wrote Desmond Ryan, 'knew the good woman well enough to practice revolver shooting in her yard, but Seán knew, and Paddy knew, that she had a pungent and scorching vocabulary when aroused. Seán, with a quiet grin, worked away with the wire, opened the window, sent Paddy to the well for water, and then lighted a fine fire. They were both half way through a good meal, which Seán had prepared, when in burst the absent housewife and met the grins of the two.

"'What divil from hell brought the pair of ye here? Only ye are who ye are, I'd knock the two heads off ye!" she shouted.'

'In August 1917,' said Tadgh Crowe, 'after his election as Sinn Féin M.P. for East Clare, Eamon de Valera visited Tipperary town on a Sunday and addressed a great gathering of people in the sports field. His visit coincided with the death of Most Rev. Dr. O'Dwyer, Bishop of Limerick, and de Valera paid tribute in his address to the patriot bishop.

'The British authorities had "proclaimed" marching in military formation, carrying hurleys and the wearing of Volunteer uniforms. All three proclamations were defied on that day. Volunteers carrying hurleys marched in military formation to the sportsfield and those who possessed uniforms wore them. Our company marched in from Solohead and, as we entered the town, "separation" women and British soldiers' dependants flung rotten eggs and various classes of filth and dirt at us. We had a bit of a scuffle with them and gave as good as we got. Otherwise the day passed off in an orderly and dignified manner. The RIC, apparently considering discretion the better part of valour, made no attempt to interfere with the parades.

'Seán Treacy was arrested a few days after this meeting and Maurice Crowe, later battalion and brigade adjutant, frequently came out to Solohead to conduct the training of the company.'

Treacy's stint in prison was shared by Eamonn O'Duibhir and Seamus O'Neill. Together they participated in a hunger strike and saw one of the most prominent of the strikers, 1916 survivor Thomas Ashe, die.

Eamonn O'Duibhir recalled the days of the hunger strike: 'Risteard O'Colmain, who had been an Easter Week fighter and who later died in Usk prison, refused, for reasons of conscience, to join the hunger strike. Because of this the Clare men tried to hound him down, but Seán [Treacy] and myself stood up to them and quashed the effort to arouse ill-feeling against O'Colmain. Seán was imbued with the spirit of fair play, and held that every Volunteer was a free man and a free agent. He was not of the type that would join the stronger side to hound down any man.'

Two days after Ashe died the prison authorities acceded to the prisoners' demands and granted them the right to have their cell doors left open from the early morning until the late evening, freedom of association, smoking privileges, parcels to be allowed in to them, an improved diet, a letter allowed in each day, and a visit a day.

In November the prisoners were moved to Dundalk Jail and, very soon, another hunger strike ensued. As a result of his deteriorating health Treacy was released; he returned to Solohead towards the end of November 1917. 'The crops on his farm at Soloheadbeg were harvested and saved during the autumn by Volunteers who gave their time freely and willingly.' said Tadgh Crowe. 'He was, however, re-arrested on 28 February 1918 and taken to Dundalk prison.'

5

THE ENIGMA OF
SEÁN TREACY

When I travelled over the scenes of Treacy's adventures in the autumn of 1939 it needed an effort to realise that he was not still living. His name was a key to open every door, a charm to take the farmer from the harvest, a power to sweep aside the lingering clouds of Civil War passion, a spell to conquer disillusion and dissipate rancour as few names in Ireland could or can.

Desmond Ryan

Who was Seán Treacy and why was he important?

Born in 1895 in Solohead, he was dead and buried in Kilfeacle churchyard by the time that he was twenty-six. His IRA friends, who stood alongside him in a combat which involved the most blistering violence, reminisced reverentially about him for the rest of their lives. People of that generation were genteel, bound by social convention, and didn't speak ill of the dead. They had nothing but good things to say about their long-dead leader.

Dying before the contradictions of age and life assailed him, Treacy represented to those who survived the Tan War an image of idealistic, brutal youth. Because he died before the Civil War seemed to spoil everything, he was idealised in their imaginations as the very essence of what a free Ireland could be and what a free Irishman should be. Therefore he emerges from history as a Robin Hood-style character, a cartoon caricature of a man; brave, kind, thoughtful, principled, egalitarian, and amusing.

He died before the deeds of the IRA were thought worthy of documentation by anyone other than their enemies in British intelligence. The main reason why he is remembered at all is because his closest guerilla comrade, Dan Breen, wrote a bestselling 1924 memoir – *My Fight for Irish Freedom* – in which Treacy is given a starring role. He was also the subject of a hagiographical biography – *Seán Treacy and the Third Tipperary Brigade* (1945) – by the redoubtable Desmond Ryan, one of the many scribes from that generation who devoted large parts of their lives to documenting Irish nationalism. If anything Ryan – whose book was once hugely popular – makes Treacy seem even more of a revolutionary saint than Breen did.

There was also a ballad about him – *Tipperary So Far Away* – which was always popular in his own county and which his fellow Tipperary men, the Clancy Brothers, successfully recorded at the height of their international 1960s fame.

In his early twenties, when his thoughts turned to armed revolution, he was a country man in charge of a small farm with two middle aged women, a domineering aunt and a worried mother, to support and protect. His neighbours respected him as a good farmer. His aunt, Mary Anne Allis, was a tough woman who wanted Treacy to concentrate on farming and to avoid the militant circles towards which he was drawn. She regarded Dan Breen as being a bad influence on her nephew. She hoped that

Treacy would 'make his way in the world.' Breen, who disliked her intensely, said that she wanted Treacy, 'to work like a nigger on the small farm that they had, and which could scarcely make a living for them.'

Treacy had a girlfriend, May Quigley, a music teacher from Dublin. He once told her aunt that, 'If you knew all about me and my doings, you might not have such a high opinion of me.'

Like Breen, he was raised without a father. When he was three his father Denis Treacy died, instigating a period of drifting which didn't stop until the family moved back to Solohead when he was eleven.

Even as a child he had to wear glasses. He had a toy rifle. 'After school hours,' said Seán Horan, 'Seán would take the man or boy his mother had in her employment out to the field where he would have a target fixed for rifle and revolver practice, and very often kept the boy firing at the target for hours at a stretch, and his aunt in a rage, having several jobs on the farm to be done of more importance to her at the time than rifle and revolver practice.'

A bookish lad, he was exceptionally enthusiastic about the Irish language and about Irish history, topics a young man with an inquiring mind would have heard little about at school back then.

One of the tales he heard around the house as a child concerned his cousin, William Allis, who had taken part in the Ballyhurst Fenian Rising. Local legend had it that Allis, still around and politically active when Treacy was a teenager, marched through Thurles with the Fenians in 1867 with a pistol in each hand. Playing on the Allis farm one day, Treacy discovered a forgotten Fenian arms dump.

The publications he subscribed to in his teens included, *Sinn Féin, Irish Freedom* and *The Irish Peasant*. He would purchase multiple copies of republican papers which he then handed out to his pals. 'Seán,' said his friend Tadgh Dwyer, 'had a mania for handing round books and papers with the advice to pass them on. He wanted to enlighten the ordinary man in the small farm houses. Seán Treacy was an out and out extremist when many of the rest of us were sympathetic enough but taking things rather easy and believing a lot of what we were told.'

Tadgh Crowe also had a living Fenian in his family. Crowe's relative, Tom Rankins of Kilfeacle, also fought at Ballyhurst. Distraught in his defeat, Rankins hopelessly pitched himself, pike in hand, against well equipped British troops. His comrades had to drag him away.

Treacy connected up with Eamonn O'Duibhir in 1911 when, aged sixteen, he attended Gaelic League Irish lessons organised by O'Duibhir. In 1911 he also joined the IRB. He was sworn in either by Eamonn O'Duibhir or Frank Drohan. He became president of the Tipperary town branch of the Gaelic League and was, in due course, made Centre of the Tipperary Circle of the IRB.

He had a dry rural sense of humour and was given to pranks and jokes. Many of his jokes were political, and have lost their sheen with the passage of time. He wrote well and, though neither terribly well read nor well educated, he was a good thinker. Dan Breen said that he was, 'away ahead of anything one might expect to meet in a country district. He had vision and to him nothing was impossible'.

He was quiet and rarely got his way within the IRA by being bellicose or bullying. He didn't play games with people and he was a straight talker. He was a conciliator who liked to win people over to his point of view through playful dialogue. He was as happy to cook breakfast for his pals as he was to lead them in battle. Seán Horan said he was 'a silent and also a sincere worker.' He didn't drink, smoke or swear.

He was five feet ten inches tall, had light blue eyes and spoke quietly. 'Seán was tall, an easy smile or a long grin showed his teeth,' said Ernie O'Malley. 'Glasses gave him a quiet appearance; he had a good strong-thrusting chin. His humour was dry enough. He dealt with men quietly. I envied him his ease; yet he never allowed slackness to pass by.'

According to O'Malley, he had an unambiguous idea of where he stood: 'In our minds Seán and I left the building up to the Irish Republic to others. They might be hostile to us, we sensed, but we knew where our sympathies were: with the labourer and small farmer in the country, the workers in the city.' When Paddy O'Dwyer, a member of Treacy's inner circle, was invited to attend a meeting organised by a socialist organisation, Treacy advised him not to attend, declaring: 'We'll use all parties and every possible means that will further the liberation of Ireland, but why should we be used by other parties?'

Breen said that he tried to form himself in the image of Michael O'Dwyer of Wicklow, a rebel who held out in the Wicklow hills after the 1798 Rising.

One of his favourite books was *The Graves of Kilmorna*, a novel concerning the Fenian Rising in Tipperary by the popular author Canon Sheehan. He read an edition of James Fintan Lalor's writings which appeared in 1918. He liked historical novels. He always carried an Irish dictionary.

His home at Solohead was maintained on a war footing, full of hidden places where he could store military equipment, ammunition and documents. Stair posts had been gouged out to create spaces where guns were hidden. Documents were concealed in the rafters. The shutters on his bedroom windows were lined with steel.

Treacy was important because he was a leader. He exerted authority with a natural grace. His analysis of the political situation as he saw it in Ireland was original, consistent, far-sighted and compelling to the young men and women who wanted to fight by his side. He was a gifted planner and analyst. He brought to guerilla warfare a remorseless spirit and a killer instinct. He was charismatic because of his integrity and reliability. Within all guerilla armies, the leaders gain their authority from their willingness to lead from the front. Treacy was always in the front line. He brought the battle to his enemy and, without putting up too much of a struggle, his enemy flinched.

'I had great confidence in Treacy,' said Tommy Ryan, related to Treacy by marriage, 'and felt that with him in command we would bring honour to our native county, Tipperary, in the fighting ahead for our national freedom.'

'Although he did not speak very much,' said Willie Myles, 'we all felt that Seán Treacy was a man of exceptional ability and courage. Though he was a great idealist, he was also a very practical idealist. Studious by nature, he went through military manuals and picked out from a great mass of material anything that would be of value to Volunteer training. As a leader he commanded the admiration of the men under him … Even at that time which was long before his fame had begun, I say we all felt that he was an exceptional leader and a great soldier and a man who, if he had not come to such an untimely end, would have risen to very great heights in military life.'

His sheer remorselessness was impressive, no matter what one thought of him.

'A Battalion Council meeting was held at Mrs Tobin's of Tincurry, at which Seán Treacy and Ernie O'Malley were present,' said Tommy Ryan. 'After the meeting Treacy and O'Malley detained me to go into some question on training details. We had just about finished our discussion when we got word to the effect that the local company had been rounded up and were all arrested. We did not know at the time what had happened, but Treacy said, "Come on! We will see what this is all about!" and we headed for the main Mitchelstown-Cahir road.

'When we reached the main road we saw on the Mitchelstown side of us, about four hundred yards away, a troop of cavalry coming towards us. There were about thirty or so of these horsemen. The prisoners, amounting to about forty, were being marched along between the files of soldiers, handcuffed in pairs. We learned afterwards that the company had been surprised at drill and the soldiers apparently had been informed where to find them, because they came prepared with handcuffs to take them in.

'When the troops were within about three hundred yards of us, the three of us opened fire on them with our pistols and revolvers. A couple of horses fell and there was a general stampede, the soldiers jumping from their horses and flying for cover. In the middle of the excitement, the prisoners cleared off, handcuffed as they were. All the Volunteers made good their escape, though some of them remained in their handcuffs for hours before they were able to get rid of them.

'This incident was one that demonstrated the character of Seán Treacy. He was full of enterprise and initiative. It was he who first suggested that we should go and see what had happened and it was he, when we saw the soldiers coming towards us with their prisoners, who decided that we should attack them.

'He was armed with his parabellum pistol; O'Malley had a Peter-the-Painter and I had a .45 Webley revolver. It was characteristic of Seán that he would take the offensive whatever the odds, and he probably realised that the surprise of our fire would be effective in concealing the weakness of our force.'

6

PRISON LETTERS

Aware that he was going to be detained and imprisoned again, Treacy chose Dinny Lacey, Maurice Crowe and Seán Duffy [shot dead by the Auxiliaries at Limerick Junction, 1921] to look after recruitment and other guerilla business during his enforced absence. He was picked up on 28 February 1918 and, once again, sent to Dundalk Jail.

Prison mates included Seamus O'Neill and the formidable Clare warrior Michael Brennan, one of three extremely capable Meelick brothers. Brennan became the commandant of the East Clare Brigade of the IRA and afterwards chief of staff of the National Army. It was Brennan who instigated the policy of refusing to recognise the authority of the court hearing his case, a symbolic contrivance used by IRA members for the next eighty years.

The three went on an immediate hunger strike to gain the right of association and other indicators of "political prisoner" status previously conceded by the prison authorities. Their protest lasted for ten days, after which they got much of what they demanded.

'Protest meetings, in connection with the treatment of the prisoners,' said Maurice Crowe, 'were held at that time at Tipperary and Solohead at which P.J. Moloney [Tipperary town chemist and Sinn Féin MP] presided, and at a meeting of the IRB it was decided to capture the sergeant of the RIC who had arrested Seán and to hold him prisoner, as a kind of hostage. This sergeant and a constable patrolled a certain railway line, but fortunately for themselves, they did not turn up on the occasion we had arranged for. Immediately following this Dan Breen and myself went to Dundalk to take part in a proposed rescue of Seán Treacy and other prisoners from the jail.'

(Writing under a pseudonym in the Clonmel *Nationalist* in 1957, the Third Tipperary Brigade's in-house historian, An tAthair Columbcille Conway, claimed that the IRB refused to sanction the proposed RIC hostage taking and that this refusal resulted in the IRB losing authority in South Tipperary. Richard Mulcahy, IRA Chief of Staff during the Tan War, wrote a lengthy refutation of this assertion in the 1969 *Capuchin Annual*

1916 participant Frank Thornton, one of Michael Collins' most trusted lieutenants, was in charge of the Dundalk Volunteers. He coordinated the planned rescue of the three hunger strikers

'We learned in Tipperary that plans for his rescue were afoot,' said Tadgh Crowe, 'and Maurice Crowe and Dan Breen left for Dundalk. I followed on the following day, staying overnight in Dublin. On the train journey from Dublin to Dundalk I had as a travelling companion a young lady whom I did not then know.

'On arrival in Dundalk, I met Maurice Crowe, Dan Breen and Frank Thornton, who was there from GHQ, and learned from them that, as Treacy and his two fellow-prisoners – Michael Brennan of Clare, and Seamus O'Neill of Cashel – had been granted their demand for treatment as political prisoners, the hunger strike was over and it was not proposed to proceed any further with the plans for the rescue.

'I called to the prison to visit Seán and, to my surprise, who was there concluding a visit to him, only my lady travelling companion? She was a Miss May Quigley and was, then or later, engaged to Seán. Breen, Maurice Crowe, Nicholas Treacy (Seán's cousin, who had also travelled up from Tipperary) and I spent that night with friendly people named McQuill in Dundalk. On my way back, I remember buying a revolver holster and belt in a shop in Capel St., Dublin.'

With the hunger strike over, Treacy resigned himself to prison life and devoted time to improving his Irish. Between visits from the likes of Breen and Maurice Crowe, he wrote a series of letters to friends and relations which give rare insights into how his mind actually worked.

He reassured his uncle Michael Allis, immediately after the strike:

'You seem to have been unnecessarily troubled about me. I didn't think you were so nervous. Of course you know by now that the strike is over. We got word this morning from [Austin] Stack. I feel just as well as ever I did. We are having great times now. Am sorry to hear of your trouble. Hope 'twill go as quick as mine went.'

In a letter to old school friend Packy Deere, a core member of his Volunteer unit since the earliest days, he wrote:

'Have just heard that you have been arrested, got three months and been removed to Cork. I suppose there is no chance of your coming here as there is no room … Do you have visits? Tell all the Cork *caílíní* [girls] I was asking for them, especially the Misses Good & Tennel.

Hope ye aren't kicking up any rows. The chief used to be civil to us. What'll the poor girl at (deleted in pencil) do after you? I suppose ye'll fix it up when you get out.

Mise,

Seán Treasaigh.'

A prison censor translated his valediction and wrote the translation down in blue pencil at the bottom of the page: 'I am, John Treacy.'

Michael Allis wrote to him again, clearly unhappy about the political involvement which seemed to be turning him into a semi-permanent prisoner. Treacy sent him an adamant reply which was intended to put an end to all family debate about his activism:

'Now I'd like you and all concerned to know, once and for ever, that I've put Ireland over all long ago, and that I will not allow my own interests or the interests of anyone else to prevent my helping her cause with all in my power. You may say this is nonsense but it is the fact. When I am released I shall at once devote all my energies to the furtherance of that cause in the best way I can.'

During one of the visits he received from Breen and Maurice Crowe he gave Crowe a bunch of keys and this extraordinarily thorough letter of instruction, dated 25 March 1918:

I meant to write to you before now, but was kept busy answering letters which arrived during the strike, including a few from Ailis

[Miss Alice Ryan]. I hope yourself, Dan and Tadgh got back from Dundalk all right. Did you get any stuff in Dublin? What a pity that rescue didn't come off, but perhaps Dan and you would be shoved in here, and I'd never stop laughing. Did you get the keys I sent you out?

The key with the bit of twine round it opens the little door at the foot of the stairs. In it you will find a few sticks of gelignite, detonators, bullets, fuse and two pikes. (Get some made like them in each company.) Also military books and note books, etc., which you can take charge of. There may be anything in the hollow pier, but I'm certain you won't find any money in it. In the note book you will find a map of Tipperary with pencil dots. The small dots are where companies already exist or can be started. The large dots, battalion centres. Thurles and Nenagh are important, but I'm sure they have these going already. Paddy Ryan will take care of Doon, but you should keep in touch with him. It will be better for you and Dinny to leave town and get the Battalion going. I think Dan has already left. Send letters under cover to James McQuill, and Miss Matthews, Dundalk, as already arranged. Will send you others later. Send me other covering addresses, as the S.S. [secret service] may suspect Ailis, No. 8. Let me know every week the progress you have made.

On 3 May 1918 he had a considerably more detailed list of instructions for Crowe, a list which outlines his entire modus operandi:

'I received all your letters safely. I am delighted at the progress ye have made. Call a meeting of the companies and elect the battalion officers, according to the Scheme of Organisation, which you will find amongst my books. Be sure and pick out the best men, and let me know. Try and get the brigade going also, especially now that so many have left work and are doing Volunteer work. I note your present H.Qrs. That is good. Keep in touch with Seamus O'Neill, as regards the Cashel area. Find out the best men in Cahir, Clonmel and Drangan.

It is now certain that the British Government intends to force conscription on this country, and the following hints will be useful.

BARRACKS:

I don't think it possible to do anything about Tipperary Military Barracks, except to try and keep them inside. Barricade all roads leading to the town with felled trees. Build stone walls across roads. Smash down bridges. Burn Station House at Tipperary, and destroy railway, wires, etc. Make all approaches to the town impassable. Snipe barracks from the surrounding hills with rifles and shotguns. Soak sods of turf in petrol, oil or tar, and throw them lighting on the huts to set them ablaze. Hit the enemy every way you can.

The companies at Donohill and Solohead should be responsible for Limerick Junction, RIC Barracks and Railway. Tear up rails, cut wires, smash down Junction Bridge, or use gelignite, if procurable. Destroy signal cabin. And also at Grange Crossing. Donaskeigh cooperate with Golden. Mount Bruis Company to be responsible for Lisvernane and Glenbane RIC Barracks, and cooperate with Galbally. Bansha to be responsible for Bansha RIC Barracks. All other Companies to be responsible for their respective Barracks, if any. The gunmen under cover should cover the windows whilst stormers smash in doors. Take the enemy by surprise. Hit first and don't let him hit you. Burn barracks. Use gelignite bombs, if procurable. Show no mercy to resisters.

RAILWAYS:

Smash stone bridges on to railway. Tear up rails at stations and throw empty trucks across lines – derail them. Smash signals. Cut telegraph and telephone wires as often as possible. Destroy signal cabins. Burn wooden bridges.

ROADS:

Barricade roads in as many places as feasible by felled trees, etc. Hold an inner line of communication intact. Defend working parties with strong guards. This is important, and at outbreak of hostilities, all lasting food stuff should be transferred to a base camp. Tinned meats, biscuits, potatoes, etc.

CAMPS:

Strongly entrench at the foot of the Galtees or any other suitable site. Dig deep in the hills for stores. Roof and prop underground chamber with timber, etc.

COMMUNICATIONS:

Open up as many new routes as you can. Slit a bicycle tube, put in despatch and mend it again. Carry a load of turnips or marigolds, cut a turnip, put in despatch, and mark turnip. Knock off a cow's horn, put in despatch, put on horn, and drive her along through the enemy. These are only ideas, but use your own judgment.

In all cases destroy a despatch before it gets into the hands of the enemy. Eat it, or get a little box in which ink is secreted, press a spring letting ink in on to the despatch. I have been thinking over the latter way and how it could be devised, but haven't it completed.

GENERAL:

Fight under cover, gunmen holding vantage points. When pike men charge, do so in close formation under cover, and then rush the enemy. Look out for aeroplanes, and don't let them catch you in close formation. Pick out your best shots with rifles to deal with them. Remember aeroplanes can easily bomb you out of houses. Deport all in favour of the enemy out of the district. Deal sternly with those who try to resist. Maintain the strictest discipline. There must be no running home to kiss mothers goodbye. Cause confusion in the enemy camp and strike terror into them.

I hope there will be no need for these instructions, but if there is, do your part and place your trust in God. Remember you can only die once and may God defend the right.

Get the men to go to Confession and Communion and remember Sarsfield, the men of 1848 and 1867, and the men of 1916.

I'm sorry I can't be with you as my term isn't up until June, but you may rest assured that we will do our part here.

Amongst the books which Treacy left with Crowe, so that he could tutor himself in revolutionary techniques, were *Cyclist Military Training, 1917*, *Field Service Pocket Book*, and *Infantry Training*.

In Treacy's absence, work went ahead in bringing together the people who would soon form the core of the feared and famous Third Tipperary Brigade of the IRA. While Treacy was locked up in Dundalk, the people who came together and followed his really detailed instructions included Breen, Con Moloney, Tadgh Crowe, Dinny Lacey, Paddy Power, three Barlow brothers (Arty, Matt, and Jack), Maurice Crowe, Con Power, Seán Fitzpatrick and Tadgh Ryan.

A brigade headquarters was established at Barlow's of Shrough. A munitions factory was started under the supervision of Dinny Lacey. A Shrough quarryman instructed the men in the handling of explosives.

When Treacy was released from Dundalk in June 1918 he discussed prison life with Breen and the two of them decided that they had never, thereafter, allow themselves to be arrested. A frenzied drive towards war began, culminating in the Soloheadbeg incident and in the all out confrontation with Britain that had been unavoidably avoided since 1848.

7

FROM REPUBLICAN BROTHERHOOD TO REPUBLICAN ARMY

Cause confusion in the enemy camp and strike terror into them.

Seán Treacy

We were attempting to instruct our people, who, with the brief exception of the Cromwellian and Williamite wars, had been disarmed since the time of Elizabeth. Most of them had never had rifles or revolvers in their hands.

Ernie O'Malley

The Soloheadbeg ambush was planned by Treacy and Breen and led by Treacy. By 21 January 1919 Seamus Robinson had been elected (at Treacy's behest) Commandant of the local Volunteers with Treacy as his deputy.

The attack is commonly cited as the event which kickstarted the Irish War of Independence. Whether it did or didn't is largely a matter of semantics but Soloheadbeg certainly represented a sea change in the direction of the dissent which had been mounting in Ireland since the Easter Rising.

With Treacy's release, he and Breen set themselves on an oppositional trajectory to the bourgeois nationalism of respectable IRB men like Pierce McCan, Eamonn O'Duibhir, and Frank Drohan. Unlike them, Treacy and Breen were not awaiting clarification or instructions from afar; if anything, they generally sought to avoid such instructions.

Soloheadbeg happened at a time when the Irish Republican (or Revolutionary) Brotherhood was turning into the Irish Republican Army (IRA). It was certainly the event which gave the IRA a baptism of fire and which instigated that organisation's guerrilla style.

On the same day as Soloheadbeg happened the Sinn Féin Members of Parliament elected in the 1918 British general election – which saw Sinn Féin eclipse the IrishParty amongst Irish nationalists – met in Dublin. They styled themselves Dáil Éireann, issued a Declaration of Independence, adopted a provisional constitution, and issued a rather progressive democratic programme.

Constables James McDonnell and Patrick O'Connell – the victims at Soloheadbeg – were, with loaded rifles, escorting a horse-drawn cart containing a consignment of gelignite from Tipperary Military Barracks to Soloheadbeg Quarry, where gelignite was needed for blasting purposes. Constable McDonnell came from Belmullet Co. Mayo. He was a widower with four children. Constable O'Connell, from Coachford Co. Cork, was single. They were accompanied by two civilians, County Council employees Patrick Quinn and Edward Godfrey.

The Volunteers who ambushed them were Paddy O'Dwyer, Seán Treacy, Seamus Robinson, Dan Breen, Seán Hogan, Tadgh Crowe, Michael Ryan, and Paddy McCormack. According to

Paddy O'Dwyer seven of the eight ambushers were armed with revolvers while Treacy bore a small automatic rifle.

Desmond Ryan, in *Seán Treacy and the Third Tipperary Brigade*, wrote that: 'Some evenings before, Constable McDonnell, who was not unpopular in the town, where he enjoyed the reputation of being a somewhat heavy wit, had asked a friend in jest: "Do you think the Sinn Féiners would shoot me? I don't think they would myself." McDonnell laughed at the notion, and with reason, as he had no enemies in particular. Nor had his companion Constable O'Connell. They were typical RIC men of the time. Little has survived of their ways and words in popular legend, except that Constable McDonnell prided himself on his skill in spelling. Many a time he questioned some company in the local taverns. "Can any man here spell rhododendron? Well, I'll tell ye: rhododendron r-h-o-d-o-d-e-n-d-r-o-n. Rhododendron!"'

Seamus Robinson afterwards claimed that Treacy and his girlfriend May Quigley came to visit him at Eamonn O'Duibhir's Kilshenane farm shortly after Christmas 1918. The purpose of their visit, he said, was to tell him about the imminent delivery of gelignite to the quarry, and to get his permission for an attack.

After the three of them had a cup of tea, Treacy and Robinson went out into the farmyard where Treacy told him about the delivery of explosives three weeks hence. Treacy advised Robinson that there could be up to six men accompanying the cart, that they would be armed, and that there was the possibility of shooting.

'Good,' Robinson remembered saying. 'Go ahead but under the condition that you let me know in time to be there myself with a couple of men from the local Battalion … men with whom I would go tiger hunting.'

Robinson claimed that Treacy asked him if they should get permission for the action from Volunteer GHQ in Dublin and that he (Robinson) replied, 'It will be unnecessary so long as we do not ask for their permission. If we ask we must await their reply.'

Breen recalled things differently, and denied that Robinson was in on the planning. Breen had a healthy disregard for Robinson and the feeling was mutual.

'Robinson was not consulted about this ambush or about the plan for it, or about a number of other things like that which were arranged,' Breen said. 'He was never told about it as something that was being done. Treacy and I had decided that we were going to shoot whatever number of police came along as an escort with this gelignite, but we did not tell Robinson anything about this.

'We had the full intention of not alone taking the gelignite they were escorting,' said Breen, 'but also of shooting down the escort, as an assertion of the national right to deny the passage of any armed enemy.'

Jerome Davin confirmed Breen's assertion that the attack was a very deliberate one. He recalled Treacy saying to him, with reference to Volunteers disinclined to violence, 'What do they think they are doing? Don't they realise that the British Army is still here? It is only when blood is shed that they will realise it.' Davin said that, after Soloheadbeg, he often discussed Treacy's words with Tadgh Dwyer and others who'd overheard him. 'We were convinced,' said Davin, 'that the taking of the gelignite was only a secondary consideration with Treacy. His real motive was to commence aggressive action against armed forces of the enemy.'

'On Tuesday 14 January 1919 I attended the fair in Tipperary town and called on Maurice Crowe ... ' said Tadgh Crowe, 'and collected from him some ammunition for a revolver which I had at the time. In accordance with instructions, I reported that night to Mrs Breen's (Dan's mother's) cottage at Donohill. I met Breen and Treacy there and the three of us went to the Tin Hut at Greenane … We were joined at the hut during the night by Seamus Robinson and Seán Hogan.'

Trusted men like Maurice Crowe, Paddy McCormack, Paddy O'Dwyer, Michael Ryan, Arty Barlow and Con Power reported to the Tin Hut – a deserted semi-derelict house – the next day. During the days that followed there were subtle changes in personnel. Many of these men had farms or other interests to look after and couldn't stay at the scene for more than a day or two. Tadgh Crowe recalled Brian Shanahan, Ned O'Reilly, Dinny Lacey, and Seán O'Meara also spending time at the Tin Hut awaiting the gelignite.

'Seán Treacy and Arty Barlow went out to cut some bushes to make a fire from a moat near at hand.' said Maurice Crowe. 'Someone remarked that it was not right to cut any wood off a moat, to which Seán replied, "Ah, sure the fairies won't say anything to us for trying to keep ourselves warm." The following morning Seán got a breakfast ready at seven o'clock. Some of us were dozing round the fire while others slept on the remains of two beds in the room – this was a disused house. He called several times that the breakfast was ready but the lads were slow in coming. When they did come they had no milk as Seán had consumed the tin of condensed milk. Of course there was general disapproval to which Seán replied, "This will show you that Volunteers must be punctual, even at breakfast!"'

It was acutely cold around Soloheadbeg at this time, with icy winds discouraging even the most ardent revolutionary spirits.

'After a week's wait,' said Tadgh Crowe, 'the whole affair ended suddenly and in a tense atmosphere. My recollection is that the two RIC men armed with carbines were walking behind the horse and cart when it came into the ambush position. There were several shouts of 'Hands up!' I myself shouted that command at least two or three times. I saw one of the policemen move up to the cart and crouch down beside it. From the position he took up and the manner in which he was handling his carbine, I was satisfied that he was going to offer resistance.'

'I was with the cart that was bringing the explosives to the Soloheadbeg quarry,' Edward Godfrey, the County Council employee, told the ensuing inquest, 'and after passing Denis Ryan's gate I was leading the horse. At the gate leading to Cranitch's field, I heard the shots; I don't know how many. I think the shots came from Cranitch's side.'

'The whole thing happened like a flash of lightning,' said Patrick Flynn.

'Robinson and I were together on the extreme left-hand side of the position, about twenty or thirty yards away from what I will call the main party of six,' said Paddy O'Dwyer, 'and the arrangements were that Robinson and I were to get out on to the road when we heard the others call on the men with the cart and the escort to stop and put up their hands, the idea being that if they did not halt, Robinson and I would be in a position to stop the horse and cart.'

Robinson claimed that Treacy and Breen, at the very last minute, insisted that they should be allowed to rush out. He thought that the RIC men were at first amused at the sight of, 'Dan Breen's burly figure with nose and mouth covered with a handkerchief; but with a sweeping glance they saw his revolver and O'Dwyer and me ... they could see only three of us.'

'Hearing Dan Breen and Seán Treacy shouting, "Halt, put up your hands!" Robinson and I immediately started to get out on to the road, and almost simultaneously either one or two shots rang out,' said Paddy O'Dwyer. 'I distinctly remember seeing one of the RIC men bringing his carbine to the aiming position and working the bolt, and the impression I got was that he was aiming at either Robinson or myself. Then a volley rang out and that constable fell dead on the roadside. I am not certain whether it was that volley or the previous shot, or shots, which killed his companion.'

'I fired three shots at him, one was ineffective and the other two got him in the arm and back,' declared Tadgh Crowe. 'About the same time, either one or two shots were fired from the gate where Seán Treacy was positioned and the other constable fell shot through the temple.'

'They came from behind me,' said Godfrey. 'I saw the two constables falling down on the road. I was on the left-hand side of the horse. Two masked men came out in front of me and held me up. They had revolvers in their hands and wore masks. There were four or five more men inside the ditch. They wore masks also. They jumped out over the ditch and took the rifles off the constables. I don't think it was the two that came in front of me that fired the shots.'

Quinn said that he, 'stepped to the right-hand side of the road, and immediately I heard the report of firearms. It seems as if they all went off together in one volley. I was greatly excited. When I looked round the two policemen were lying on the ground. There was only one burst of firing altogether. They took away the rifles the police had, and the ammunition. I had a view of the cart … one of the masked men led it away, only for a short distance, as there was a bend on the road. They went away like a shot, just as fast as they had come. They all went away with the horse. One of them led the horse by the head. I did not know what happened. I was so excited.'

Paddy O'Dwyer remembered that Godfrey and Quinn were terrified by the shooting and killing going on around them: 'Dan Breen spoke to them and told them that nothing was going to happen to them. One of these men, Godfrey, knew both Breen and Treacy well, and I imagine that Flynn [sic] must have known them too. On Breen's instructions, Tadgh Crowe and I collected the two carbines belonging to the dead constables. Breen, Treacy and Hogan then drove away the horse and cart with the gelignite.'

Robinson, twenty years after the events, told Desmond Ryan that, 'It was untrue to say that our enemies at Soloheadbeg did not get "a dog's chance". Neither Seán Treacy, nor I, nor Dan Breen, nor any of us would have shot down men in cold blood, although certainly we had no intention of being intimidated by the armed guard.'

'Treacy, Breen, and Hogan drove away on the horse and cart with the gelignite,' said Tadgh Crowe, 'and Paddy O'Dwyer and I took the RIC men's carbines and hid them together with the belts, pouches of ammunition, and handcuffs in a ditch about half a mile from the scene of the ambush. O'Dwyer and I then parted, he to go back home to Hollyford, and I went to Doherty's of Seskin. After having some tea in Doherty's, I returned home and told my father that he might expect raids by the police. In fact, I told him exactly what was after happening. We discussed the matter for a few minutes and he advised me to go away at once, but warned me against staying in the houses of relatives as, he said, if the police were looking for me they would be sure to trace and raid the homes of all our relations.

'I stayed that night with two old men, very distant relations of my family, and next day I went back towards my home. My sister met me near the house and brought me some food. She told me that RIC men from Tipperary had raided the house looking for me at about 6 p.m. on the previous night, and that my father had told them I was not back from the fair in Mitchelstown. They raided again, she said, about midnight and again in the early hours of that morning. That news dispelled any thoughts I may have had about returning home, and I continued on the run for the following two and a half years until the Truce came in July 1921.'

'Seán Treacy had made all the arrangements for disposing of the gelignite,' said Robinson. 'Dan Breen and Seán Hogan mounted the cart. Breen, standing up with the reins, whipped the horse and away they went clattering on the rough road.'

'I would like to make this point clear,' Breen told the Bureau of Military History over thirty years later and for the benefit of potential historians, 'and state here without any equivocation that we took this action deliberately having thought the matter over and talked it over between us. Treacy had stated to me that the only way of starting a war was to kill someone and we wanted to start a war, so we intended to kill some of the police whom we looked upon as the foremost and most important branch of the enemy forces which were holding our country in subjection. The moral aspect of such a decision has been talked about since and we have been branded as murderers, both by the enemy and even by some of our own people, but I want it to be understood that the pros and cons were thoroughly weighed up in discussions between Treacy and myself and, to put it in a nutshell, we felt that we were merely continuing the active war for the establishment of the Irish Republic that had begun on Easter Monday 1916 … The only regret we had, following the ambush was that there were only two policemen in it instead of the six we expected, because we felt that six dead policemen would have impressed the country more than a mere two.'

When May Quigley's aunt later suggested to Treacy that Constable McDonnell was an elderly and harmless man with a family, Treacy replied that 'It was regrettable, but it was unavoidable.'

As a result of Soloheadbeg, Treacy, Breen, Robinson and Hogan were thereafter known by their supporters as the Big Four.

'I did not actually know anything about the projected attack at Soloheadbeg,' said Tommy Ryan, 'but on the day it occurred I got a message from Treacy informing me that it had taken place and that they, the attacking party, intended to stay at my place that night. As it happened, there was a threshing machine* coming to our place on the same evening to begin threshing operations the following day which, of course, brought a lot of people around the place. There was also a strong rumour current that I was about to be arrested as a result of my appearing in command and drilling Volunteers openly at Clogheen a short time before that. I left my own house that evening to meet Treacy, Breen and Seamus Robinson at Tincurry but, when I arrived there, I was told that they had changed their plans. I then returned home. On the following morning my home was raided by six RIC men and I was arrested.

I was tried in Clogheen Court that day and sentenced to three months' imprisonment. Discussing this afterwards with Breen and Treacy, they remarked that it would have been a bad job for the RIC if they had carried out their original intention to stay with me on that night. They would have attacked the raiding party the moment they appeared.'

A few days after the killings the RIC called on an elderly relative of Seán Hogan's. Assuring the old man that no harm would come to young Hogan if he gave himself up, they handed him the flyer which advertised a £1000 reward being offered for the capture of the Soloheadbeg conspirators. To their surprise the old man took the flyer from them and seemed to be giving it his entire attention. After a silent pause he handed it back to the officer and said, 'Well, sergeant, there is one thing certain. It was a scholar wrote that!'

During the summer of 1919 Treacy and Jerome Davin from the Third Tipperary Brigade experimented with some of the captured gelignite. 'It was then that the idea of what later became known as "mud bombs" occurred to us,' said Davin. 'The idea was simply a stick of gelignite moulded in sticky yellow clay and ignited by a fuse and detonator. We first tried it out on an old vacant house. The sticky yellow clay held the gelignite in position on the roof and the explosives blew a circular hole in the roof of the house. Treacy was delighted with the result and I remember him remarking to me at the time: "This, Jerome, will be part of our equipment for attacks on RIC barracks." I mention this so that the reader may have an idea of how Treacy was always looking ahead. At that time (the summer of 1919) few contemplated that within a year attacks on RIC barracks would be a feature of IRA activity. Later we discovered that a coat of linseed oil on the yellow clay gave it a greater tackiness and made the bombs adhere better to slate roofs.'

On Sunday 11 May 1919 a late night dance took place at Kilshenane. Host Eamonn O'Duibhir said that, 'the young and the brave and the beautiful from the countryside were there in great numbers. Seán Ó Treasaigh, Seán Hogan, Seamus Robinson, and, I think, Dan Breen were there. We were all there.'

Mick Davern from the Second Tipperary Brigade, who went on to found a Tipperary Fianna Fail dynasty, witnessed the events leading up to the arrest of Seán Hogan and his rescue at Knocklong, an episode which had about it all the adventure of a Hollywood movie. Soloheadbeg had not been universally popular – it caused considerable unease. Knocklong, a bona fide tale of fierce resoluteness, went down well with the IRA's natural constituencies.

Davern was given the difficult task, by Treacy, of keeping the flirtatious Hogan on a leash. 'Seamus, Dan, Seán and J.J. [Seán Hogan] and about seventy or eighty couples attended the dance which was under a heavy guard and covered by excellent scouting. The dance continued without incident until 5 a.m.... I had been keeping company with Mary O'Brien of Rossmore who was a prominent Cumman na mBan* girl for some years, and Seán Hogan was in love with Bridie O'Keefe of Glenough. Hogan intimated to me that he was returning with me to Rossmore. I informed Seán Treacy, who warned me "Don't leave him out of your sight and I will wait for ye at Lacey's Cross." – which was near Glenough. I pumped Hogan's bike and the four of us proceeded towards the village of Ballagh. When we got there Hogan asked me for the pump again, I handed it to him; he put it his pocket and said: "Tell the boys I'll be in Glenough about four this evening." I argued with him and told him of my promise to Seán Treacy and tried to get hold of his bike, but he jumped on it shouting, "Two is company, three is a crowd.'"

For the first time in his life Davern dreaded his next meeting with Treacy, where he would have to explain things. When they met, Treacy, known for his even temper, was visibly exasperated. He said he would have disciplinary action taken against Hogan and fumed that this was not Hogan's first breach of authority. 'This is not your fault, Mick,' he said to Davern, 'and this is not the first time he did such things. I will teach him sense when I get hold of him.'

On 12 May Hogan was advised, as he breakfasted and relaxed in the farmhouse where he had stayed overnight, that there was about to be a raid. A party of RIC was approaching with the intention of making a low-key inspection of the farmhouse, as opposed to hunting for one of the Soloheadbeg gang.

Hogan proceeded to walk directly into, instead of escaping from, the search party. Transferred to Thurles, he was interrogated there and, eventually, recognised as being one of the notorious 'Soloheadbeg Murder Gang'. Security was tightened around him as plans were made to transfer him to Cork.

When Robinson, Treacy and Breen heard of Hogan's arrest, and that he was being held in Thurles, they made an immediate decision to rescue him. It was predictable that Hogan would very soon be transferred by train to Cork. They determined that they had free him while he was in transit on that train.

Assistance was sought while they set about choosing a suitable train station at which to stage the rescue. Goold's Cross, Emly and

Knocklong were considered to be suitably small and unguarded. Goold's Cross was station-of-choice to the Third Tipperary Brigade and Treacy often had to shoot his way out of there when returning to his region from Dublin.

High drama which didn't happen at Goold's Cross tended to happen at Limerick Junction. Michael Collins, when he wanted to meet local IRA men on the ground, would often arrange to meet them in the waiting room at Limerick Junction. Massey the traitor had been arrested in the same waiting-room during the Fenian Rising.

Treacy established a mission headquarters not far from Emly. There, in the early hours of 13 May, Robinson, Breen, and Treacy worked out their plan. Treacy fretted about which station would prove the best bet, which would be furthest from RIC and Army reinforcements, which would allow the greatest hope of a getaway.

Emly and Knocklong, being in Co. Limerick, were outside the Tipperary men's Brigade area. There were friendly ties between the east Limerick and South Tipperary IRA – they regularly co-operated on important jobs – but the Galbally Brigade, within whose area the rescue was to be attempted, were territorial enough. They were happy to allow the Big Three across their borders so that they could rescue their pal but they baulked at allowing virtual hordes of Tipperary fighters into their space. It was agreed that the Galbally Battalion would supply enough men and whatever else was needed for the job.

At Emly the decision was finally made – they would rescue Hogan at Knocklong. The countryside around Knocklong was quiet and, on one side of the station, deserted. The two nearest barracks were more than three miles away.

Women and men set about watching Thurles barracks, train station, and points in between there and Knocklong. Coded telegrams would be used to convey news of Hogan's movements.

'On the evening of 12 May 1919,' said Thurles Cumman na mBan member Bridget Ryan, 'I received through the usual channels a despatch from Michael Collins with a covering note addressed to me personally, telling me that the despatch was extremely urgent and requesting me to have it forwarded to the destination at once. I have an idea that the despatch was for Seán Treacy, but of that I am not now quite certain. I immediately gave it with the covering note to McCormack [John McCormack, Mid Tipperary IRA] who took it at once to Micksey O'Connell's shop.

'What transpired in O'Connell's shop, or who besides Micksey O'Connell met there, I do not know but, on his return, McCormack told me that Seán Hogan, who was wanted by the RIC, in connection with the Soloheadbeg ambush, had been arrested in the early hours of that morning at Maher's of Annefield and that he [Hogan] was a prisoner in the RIC barracks in Thurles. Continuing, McCormack told me it was expected that Hogan would be sent to Cork prison under escort by some of the trains during the day, that arrangements had been made to watch the barracks, and that if Hogan was being sent to Cork it had been decided that Micksey O'Connell would send a code telegram, worded "Greyhound on train" and giving the time of the departure of the train, to: Shanahan, Coal Stores, Knocklong. McCormack asked my permission to use my name as the sender of the telegram which I readily and willingly gave. I did not at that time know Shanahan's of Knocklong nor did it occur to me at the time to suggest to McCormack to use a fictitious name, and I expect in the hurry and with all McCormack and O'Connell had to do that day it did not occur to them either.

'Throughout the day the barracks was constantly watched by an elderly lady named Mrs McCarthy, her daughter Margaret and a Miss Maher of Annefield (now Mrs Frank McGrath of Nenagh) at whose house Hogan had been arrested and who had followed the police into Thurles. They made several efforts to secure a visit to the prisoner, each time pleading to be allowed to see him for a few minutes, but the RIC were definite in their refusal. These visits, however, provided Mrs McCarthy with the excuse which she required to remain in the vicinity of the barracks for long intervals. Eventually, that evening, Mrs McCarthy secured the information that Hogan was being taken to Cork by a train which left Thurles round about 6 p.m. and, when she reported this to Micksey O'Connell, Micksey sent what later became the famous telegram.'

At 1.29 p.m. the morning train from Dublin pulled into Knocklong. Hogan's pals went on board but found no sign of him. The three then returned to Emly and prepared to meet the evening train, due into Knocklong at 8 p.m.. Five Galbally IRA men were recruited and the plan was given some last minute fine tuning.

As the Cork-bound train made its way south, four Galbally Volunteers got on board at Emly, the stop which preceded Knocklong. They soon discovered that Hogan was on the train, guarded by four armed RIC men.

They were to warn the Knocklong rescuers – Breen, Robinson, Treacy, and Eamonn O'Brien, a Galbally man closely linked to the Big Four – that Hogan was there and to indicate exactly which compartment he was held in.

Hogan sat in a compartment, handcuffed and seated between Sergeant Wallace and Constable Enright. Both men carried revolvers. Opposite Hogan there were two other Constables, Ring and Reilly, bearing shotguns.

Treacy and Eamonn O'Brien walked down to Knocklong station, while Breen and Robinson entered the town on bikes. Breen and Robinson were to linger around the station entrance, acting as lookouts, while O'Brien and Treacy went in to free Hogan.

When the train pulled into the station, two of the Galbally men jumped out before it ground to a halt. One of them pointed to the compartment where Hogan sat under guard. Treacy and O'Brien strode onto the train, revolvers drawn.

They made their way to Hogan's compartment, thrust open its sliding door, and shouted, 'Hands up! Come on Seán, out!' Constable Enright placed a revolver against Hogan's neck and crouched in behind him for cover. Treacy and O'Brien opened fire, killing Enright. 'We certainly would never have fired if Enright had not made a move to attack Hogan,' O'Brien later maintained.

Hogan jumped up and crashed his handcuffed hands right into the face of Constable Ring, sitting opposite him. Treacy and Wallace wrestled viciously with one another, while Eamonn O'Brien and Constable Reilly fell into a similar struggle. Then the Galbally contingent stormed onto the train virtually unarmed and wrenched Reilly's rifle away from him. One of them smashed him across the head with his own weapon and he collapsed onto the floor, apparently knocked out. Constable Ring either jumped out a window or was thrown out through it. This was the last that was seen or heard of him for some time.

Treacy, still wrestling with Wallace, told Hogan to leave the train. The teenager withdrew, with difficulty, as far as the corridor. There were now so many people in the small compartment that chaos reigned. While the tenacious Wallace and the resolute Treacy remained locked in combat, Treacy repeatedly appealed to the powerfully built Sergeant to give it up but one man was as stubborn as the other.

Wallace was now getting the upper hand in his struggle with Treacy. The two were grappling desperately for control of Wallace's Webley revolver, whose barrel was remorselessly turning in the direction of Treacy's head. Eamonn O'Brien fired at Wallace just as the policeman put a bullet through Treacy's neck.

Wallace fell back, mortally wounded. The rescue party was in a position to get off the train. Treacy had little fight left in him, he told a friend, 'I thought I was a dead man. I had to hold my head up with both hands, but I knew I could walk.'

Wallace was an important political officer, his pre-eminence shown by the fact that he was in charge of a key prisoner like Hogan. According to local chatter he had been cursed from the pulpit by a priest. Seamus Malone knew the root of that story. When he had married Gaelic League organiser Brigid Walsh, back in 1917, the RIC tried to arrest him; 'The police stopped the motor car at the crossroads, but I wasn't in it. They raced back to the church but the old priest put the run on them. I had left but the priest did not know that. He warned Sergeant Wallace, who was in charge of the police, that the bad work of the morning would not do him any good. When Wallace was killed on the train at Knocklong, in 1919, many people in Drumbane remembered the words of the priest. Probably only a complaint about the business, or something of that kind, was all the priest had in mind, but the story tellers of Drumbane are convinced that it was the deaf old priest's talk which encompassed the death of Wallace.'

As they made to leave the station they heard a shotgun going off. Constable Reilly had either feigned unconsciousness or was rapidly coming round. According to the *Tipperary Star*: 'when he recovered from the staggering jab he had received in the affray, he dashed out firing shots like a man entirely out of his senses. The stationmaster, amongst others, had a narrow shave from random bullets.'

Breen and Robinson rushed onto the platform, Breen firing fiercely at Reilly with an accuracy which forced him to withdraw, taking pressure off the retreating rescuers. Reilly hit Breen twice during their fight, one bullet going through Breen's lung, the other injuring his arm. Treacy tottered on the edge of unconsciousness, Breen was delirious with pain, and Hogan was still handcuffed.

As the injured men were dragged away, Hogan rushed into a butcher's shop and shouted at the startled butcher, 'Take them off! Take them off!' as he held up his hands. The butcher's wife bolted the shop door, got a seven pound weight with a deep groove in it, and told Hogan to place his hands over the centre bar of the weight. Her husband took his meat cleaver and, with one good belt, broke the handcuffs. Hogan was then guided out through the back door of the house and pointed in the direction of open country. He soon caught up with the others.

Hogan had faced almost certain execution in Cork. His daring escape from the jaws of the enemy enervated the inhabitants of Tipperary, Cork, and Limerick. Knocklong marked a turning point in the embryonic revolution, being its first genuinely popular action.

Hogan was a good-looking boyish character popular with the many girls who came into contact with him at the various dances and social occasions which he attended. He was just two days short of his eighteenth birthday. His liberation was a profoundly dramatic affray. It had the effect of mobilising support for the IRA, of lending to them a glamorous vagabond image.

'The police,' says Joost Augusteijn, 'reported that the killings at Knocklong were kindly received by the population.' Particularly, the RIC County Inspector reported, 'in parts of Tipperary and Cashel, districts peculiarly given to this form of showing hatred to constituted authority.'

The rescue became the subject of many ballads and fireside tales. Seán Hogan became, temporarily, one of the most famous men in Tipperary:

The news had spread thru Ireland and spread from shore to shore
Of such a deed no living man has ever heard before,
From out of guarded carriages 'mid the panic-stricken throng,
Seán Hogan he was rescued at the Station of Knocklong.

Munster grew too hot for the Big Four and, for a while, they concentrated their efforts on the Dublin area. Breen and Treacy began commuting back and forth between Dublin and Tipperary. Shortly after they arrived in the capital city they had a vaguely fraught meeting with Chief of Staff Richard Mulcahy, who plainly didn't want Treacy and Breen to remain in Dublin.

'Mulcahy advanced a certain line of argument as to why we should allow ourselves to be smuggled away to America,' said Breen, 'We told him against that, that we had no intention of leaving the country, to which he replied that, if we persisted in staying here, we would be disobeying the ruling of the General Staff. He pointed out that the General Staff could not allow itself to be pushed into war before it was ready to take such action itself and that our action at Soloheadbeg and Knocklong, having been taken entirely on our own responsibility, could not be stood over by GHQ. He said that, if we insisted in staying in the country and if we were arrested or killed by the enemy, GHQ could not acknowledge us as acting with authority and that we would, therefore, be branded as murderers. I said that we realised all that, but that we still intended to stay here and to carry on the fight we had begun, following which Mulcahy then made the extraordinary suggestion that, if we persisted in remaining, GHQ had authorised him to offer us a payment of £5 a week to keep us. To this offer I replied that, if we were to be considered as murderers, at least we would not justify the name of paid murderers, and that our friends, who had been so kind as to keep us all this time, would no doubt continue to do so.'

The Tipperary gang stayed with their friends in a variety of north Dublin houses and hostelries. One such reliable bolthole was The Crown Hotel run by Annie Farrington who ended her days as the proprietor of Barry's Hotel, an enduring republican bastion for the next fifty years. 'Dan Breen stayed at the Crown several times,' Farrington said. 'He had various people with him from time to time; Seán Treacy, Seán Hogan and others whose names I did not know. On one occasion about six or seven of them came and they were in a dreadful condition. They had been sleeping inside the walls surrounding some church for several nights and had a few days growth of beard. Dan begged me to give them some sort of a shakedown. The hotel was full of guests and I went and took some of the mattresses from the beds and placed them on the drawing-room floor, leaving the guests with only the box springs. They only stayed one night. I fed everyone who came in like that.'

Mulcahy, despite his personal reservations, soon had to bow to the will of others – Collins wanted Treacy, Breen and their sidekicks at hand.

At the end of his life Mulcahy was still telling his son that events like Soloheadbeg had, 'pushed rather turbulent spirits such as Breen and Treacy into the Dublin arena from time to time where their services were not required and their presence was often awkward.'

'Troublesome spirits' were exactly what Collins wanted for the group of men who became known as the Squad or the Twelve Apostles. This urban flying column, principally made up of working class Dublin Volunteers, came under the control of Collins' Intelligence Department. The Squad specialised in the execution of British intelligence agents and policemen who were particularly diligent or arrogant in their dealings with the IRA. Mick McDonnell was their first leader, with Paddy Daly as his second in command. Daly later eclipsed McDonnell.

According to Joe Leonard, a close associate of Collins' and one of the most active members of the Squad, this counter-intelligence cell started in September 1919 when Mulcahy summoned a number of exceptionally intrepid Volunteers to a meeting at Parnell Square, Dublin. The IRA leadership was represented by Collins, Dick McKee (commandant, Dublin Brigade), Peadar Clancy (vice commandant, Dublin Brigade) and Mick McDonnell.

Mulcahy, said Leonard, explained that the purpose of the meeting was to tell the men of the urgent need for vigorous action, 'against the British executive and political detectives who were harassing Dáil Éireann and our Headquarters staff.'

The founding members of the Squad at this meeting were asked if they were prepared to give their entire time and thought to this new mission. Joe Leonard thought that the men present in Parnell Square were himself, Seán Doyle, Paddy Daly, Ben Barrett, and, 'the four Tipperary men from the Knocklong job – Seán Treacy, Dan Breen, J.J. Hogan, and Seamus Robinson – to be attached for a time.'

Paddy Daly told Desmond Ryan that Treacy, 'always came readily to help us, and his attitude always was "What can we do to help? Here we are!"' Collins had trusted and valued Treacy ever since their first meeting after Soloheadbeg. It was well known that Treacy could cajole or charm Collins into giving him additional arms and ammunition.

While the Big Four concentrated their efforts temporarily on Dublin, Jerome Davin was, with Maurice Crowe, one of the men who kept the IRA campaign going back home. He visited Dublin sporadically to liaise with GHQ. 'On one occasion,' said Davin, 'Michael Collins gave me a message for a family named Fitzgeralds of Ballydrehid, Cahir. We had been trying to trace a boy of the Fitzgeralds who was in Dublin at the time of the Rising in 1916 and who had been missing from that time. Collins had been unable to trace him and I was to inform his family that he was still missing and believed killed in the rising. Later I believe the boy turned up down in some part of the west of Ireland.'

Lord John French was the King's representative in Ireland and the day-to-day ruler of the island. An army officer back from the Great War, he gradually introduced into Ireland a succession of aggressive military methods which effectively hampered the escalating insurgency. Collins was determined to assassinate him on both practical and public relations grounds. There were at least twelve serious attempts to kill him, and Volunteers from the country were regularly recruited for these endeavours

Breen could recall four or five occasions when arrangements were made to ambush French, for all of which the old soldier failed to turn up: 'We all arranged to stay somewhere that we could be easily reached by phone, but Robinson, who was staying in Heytesbury St, could not be contacted by phone. So I went on one of these occasions to warn him of a proposed attack, but he informed me that he was having nothing to do with it and that he was not taking part in any more of these Dublin exploits. I told Treacy about this and actually we did get him to come with us to Ashtown.'

The Ashtown attack had, of necessity, to be organised at short notice. Squad associate Vinnie Byrne was socialising on the night of 18 December 1919 when he heard, via the son of a train guard, that Lord French was due to travel up to Dublin from Roscommon the following morning. Byrne asked his companion what time his father – who was working on French's train – would get back to Dublin, and the son told Byrne that the father would be home around eleven or twelve o'clock in the morning.

'I immediately went to Mick McDonnell's house, which was in Richmond Crescent, and reported to him what I had heard,' said Byrne. 'Mick said: "That's the best bit of news I've had for a long

We proudly remember our Comrade and great leader Sean O Treasaigh, V.O.C., 3rd Tipp Brigade whose courage and example inspired his generation in the Anglo-Irish War, 1916—1921.

We also proudly remember all our Comrades of the Brigade who have passed on to their eternal reward since 1923, whose names are too many to record here. Ar Dheis De go Raibh siad uiligh.

seán ó cᴚeasaiᵹ

Caoiseac i naᴚm poblact na héiᴚeann. a cuic i ᵹcac i ᵹcoinnib fóᴚsaí na sasanac i mbaile áca cliac. 14 ᴅeiᴚe-fóṁaiᴚ, 1920

We salute your memory in this the 50th anniversary year of your death in Dublin

Born in the parish of Solohead, Tipperary, 14th February, 1895. From an early age dedicated his life to Ireland's freedom. An Irish language enthusiast and organiser, he also organised the Irish Volunteers in County Tipperary and was their outstanding leader. His deeds of daring in the Anglo-Irish War would fill volumes. His decision to resume guerrilla warfare at Soloheadbeg on 21st January, 1919, was the most significant event since the Easter Rising, resulting ultimately in the freedom we have today. He died in battle against British forces in Talbot Street, Dublin, 14th October, 1920, and is interred in Kilfeacle churchyard. His name and fame will never fade : His heroic spirit still lives on.

We recall wi[...] your valiant [...] the Fight f[...] Freedo[...]

THIRD TIPPERARY BRIGADE — ROLL OF HONOUR, 1916—1923
Officers and men who gave their lives for the Fight for Freedom.

1st Batt.
(Rosegreen area) :
Tom Lee
Jerry Lyons
Tom Larkin

2nd Batt.
(Golden area) :
Pierce McCann
Paddy Hogan
Lar Luby
P. Delaney
Patrick Lynch

3rd Batt.
(Dundrum area) :
Dan Carew
Martin Purcell
Jack Ryan (Master)
Mick Ryan (Patsy)
P. Dwyer (Bradshaw)
D. O'Dwyer (M)
Peter Maher
Seamus Quirke

4th Batt.
(Tipp. Town area) :
Sean Treacy
Sean Duffy
Pat Moloney
Frank O'Dwyer
Ned O'Dwyer
Willie Ryan
W. Crowe
Bill O'Brien
Jim Hickey
Mick Edmonds
Sean Allen
Tom Looby
Jack Hayes
Jim O'Meara
Jerry Riggs
Con Hanley
Pake Dalton
James O'Connor
Martin Breen
Denis Ryan
Denis Lacy
Paddy McDonagh
Jerry Kiely
Mick Fitzgerald
Jack Riordan
Michael Hartnett

6th Batt.
(Cahir area) :
S. O'Mahony
Patrick English
Tom O'Dea

7th Batt.
(Drangan area) :
Patrick Hackett
Jim Hayes
S. Brett
M. Ryan
S. Quinn
Dick Fleming
M. O'Neill
P. Bennett
Jim Egan
Tom Donovan
Denis Sadlier
Mick Sadlier
Ned Somers
M. Heffernan
Paddy Clancy
Martin Clancy

5th Batt.
(Clonmel area) :
Jim O'Keeffe
Frank O'Keeffe
Mick McGrath
Michael Condon
Theo English

8th Batt.
(Carrick area) :
L. O'Neill
S. Tobin
P. Dalton
P. Neachton
S. Browne
R. Meagher
Maurice McGrath
Michael Hogan
S. St. John
Tom Kennedy
T. Torpey
Pat Butler
Ned Butler
P. O'Hanlon
Pat Quinlan

Go ndeanaigh Dia trochaire ortha uiligh.

Published by the Commemoration Committee, 1970
Printed by Fitzpatrick Bros. Tipperary.

IRA intelligence photograph of RIC men and their best friend.

Mick O'Callaghan.
Treacy thought O'Callaghan
saved Tipperary's good name
during 1916.

Sean Hogan.
Rescued at Knocklong,
leader of the No. 2 Flying
Column.

Ned O'Dwyer.
Third Tipperary Brigade and
No. 2 Flying Column.

Price 6d

OFFICIAL SOUVENIR

OF THE

SOLOHEADBEG MEMORIAL

Commemorating the Ambush at Soloheadbeg, 21st January, 1919.

Erected at Solohead Cross, Tipperary.

Unveiled by The President of Ireland,
seán c. ó ceallaiġ,
On Sunday, 22nd January, 1950.

The unveiling of the Soloheadbeg memorial, shunned by Seamus
Robinson and the local bishop, proved as controversial as the event it
commemorated.

Thomas Lee.
Third Tipperary Brigade.
Killed near Fethard, following a
raid by British troops in
March 1921.

Dinny Lacey.
Leader of the No.1 Flying
Column. Fought alongside Tom
Barry in the Civil War. Killed in
the Glen of Aherlow, 1923.

From left: Seamus Robinson, Sean Hogan, Sean Treacy, Dan Breen,
and Mick Brennan. Clare IRA leader Brennan did jail time with Treacy.

From left: Ned Reilly, the maverick Paddy Ryan Lacken, and Jimmy Leahy.

From left: Sean Hogan, Dan Breen, Ned Reilly. Reilly was involved in the Knocklong incident and in barracks attacks.

Cashel members of the Third Tipperary Brigade.

British tank in Fethard.

Taken during IRA training session, includes Mossy McGrath
(back row, first on left) and Dick Dalton (middle row, last on right,
crouching).

Mick Hogan. Tipperary footballer and IRA member killed during Bloody Sunday.

Ticket for Bloody Sunday football match.

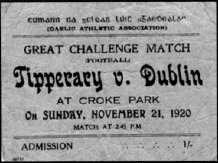

IRA transportation *(Photo courtesy of Carrie Acheson)*

Lancia armoured car and Crossley Tender abandoning Thurles RIC
Barracks at the end of the Tan War.

time." The next thing he said was: "You had better be here in the morning at about ten o'clock, as we might have a go on French."'

The following morning Byrne reported back to McDonnell's house on time. There was a group of men waiting in the front room. He already knew Martin Savage (a handsome young Sligo man who'd been in the GPO in 1916), Tom Keogh (an expert marksman), Paddy Daly, and Joe Leonard. McDonnell introduced him to the others: Breen, Robinson, Treacy, and Hogan. This group headed by bike to Ashtown Road, where they knew that French would be disembarking from his train.

'We halted at Kelly's pub,' said Byrne, 'Mick McDonnell, Dan Breen, Seán Treacy and Paddy Daly stood in a group and were having a conversation together. After a few minutes we all went into the pub. Minerals, as far as I remember, were ordered. When I had finished my glass, Mick called me and told me to get my bike, cycle towards the station, and see if there was any sign of the train, or if there were any military or police there … I had only gone about two hundred yards when I heard the sound of motor cars behind me. A motor horn sounded and I pulled into the side and let them pass. There were four cars in all. I wheeled round, cycled back as hard as I could and reported to Mick McDonnell about the military passing me going to the station.'

They began, at that moment, to hear French's train approaching. Daly, Leonard, Robinson, Treacy and Hogan went to the back yard of the pub, making their way into a field where they took up positions behind a hedge which looked out over the station road.

McDonnell, Breen and Keogh commandeered a large farm cart in the yard and attempted to move it out onto the road. The cart proved heavier than expected and it got stuck. At that moment two traffic police showed up on foot, heading in the direction of the station. The ambushers scarcely had time to register their presence when they heard the convoy of cars coming from the station. Before they knew it, French and his protectors were drawing perilously near.

As the cars approached, the men behind the hedge opened fire with revolvers and grenades. 'The first car to come was a dark blue one,' said Byrne, 'Sitting beside the driver was a man in civilian clothes who, we learned afterwards, was Detective Officer Nalley. He was firing from a revolver. As the car came clear of the corner, I let fly a grenade which hit the back of the car and exploded. The next thing I saw was the peeler being blown across the road. The second car was stopped right opposite to our men behind the hedge. This car was a closed one, khaki-green in colour. The third car was a box Ford type, with a canvas roof, which flew by with a continuous fire on it. The fourth car which came along was an open Sunbeam car and in it were a soldier driver and a sergeant. The sergeant was lying across the back of the car and firing from a rifle. Where we were standing we were an open target for him. In fact you could hear the bullets whistling by, finding a billet in the wall behind us. As this car was disappearing around the wide bend of the road leading to the Ashtown Gate of the Phoenix Park, I heard Martin Savage saying something, and it sounded like this: "Oh, lads, I am hit." The next moment he was dead, lying on the road.'

The driver of the khaki-green car climbed out of his vehicle waving a handkerchief. McDonnell accepted his surrender and asked him where Lord French was. The soldier – Corporal Appleby – said that the Lord Lieutenant had been blown to pieces in his car. Appleby's false information was accepted, in the heat of battle, at face value. In reality French got away unscathed. Some of the ambushers wanted to shoot Appleby but McDonnell decided to let him go. Breen's leg had been injured, and he was bleeding a lot.

Treacy and Robinson remained behind while all the others made their getaway by bike. Robinson, preparing to depart, found that his own bike had been badly damaged in the melee. Treacy gave him a lift on his cycle and they slowly made good their escape until they came across a retired RIC man out for a ride on his brand new bicycle. They commandeered it with the promise that it would be left, for collection, at a certain place in the city that evening. They then moved on to Dolphin's Barn.

Treacy and Breen were still actively hunting down prime targets in Dublin, but diligently looking after training down in Tipperary, when Ernie O'Malley encountered Treacy in the spring of 1920. It was O'Malley's job to knock the IRA into shape for the anticipated battles ahead. 'I met Seán Treacy's grin as he cycled past on a bicycle,' O'Malley wrote in *On Another Man's Wound*. 'He had grown a thin moustache since I had met him with Breen and Robinson in North Tipp. Seamus Robinson was given to pedalling also. Both were on intelligence work; they were helping to reduce the number of detectives. "We asked Michael Collins to send you to South Tipp," said Seán. "He told us that Kerry had asked for you, but we'll wear him down and we'll go back with you".'

Shortly afterwards, having discussed the pros and cons of various Kerry IRA officers with O'Malley, Collins told him that he was being sent to Tipperary. Treacy had got his way. When O'Malley reached Tipperary town Treacy and Robinson were already waiting there to greet him. They had fought their way through a police line in order to reach the town on time.

To O'Malley South Tipperary represented optimum guerilla warfare territory. The lay of the land combined with an overabundance of enemy targets and a motivated local IRA leadership. 'The Brigade ran from East Limerick to the Kilkenny border beyond Carrick-on-Suir,' he remembered in *On Another Man's Wound*. 'On the south it was cut off by the Knockmealdown, Monavullagh and Comeragh mountains; on the north were the hills above Hollyford, the plain of the Golden Vale and the Slieveardagh hills beyond Killenaule. There were eight battalions. South Tipperary lay across communications with the lower Shannon and the south-west. The land was fertile, there was hardly any bog and roads were numerous. Mountains rose sheer out of the plain as massives and the land close to the mountains, unlike that in Donegal or North Tipp., was good.

'There were strong military barracks at Tipperary, Cahir, Clonmel, Cashel and Fethard. There were independent posts as well and police barracks. Tipperary town had over one thousand troops between the barracks, rifle range and hutments, and Royal Irish Constabulary.'

He felt that it was good to have with him at this time two men – Treacy and Robinson – who could think and act for themselves, and who were prepared to fight. 'They were good shots and without fear,' O'Malley wrote, 'we discussed the nature of the country, training, and operations continuously, as we walked or cycled. I wanted to visit each battalion first, and then plan operations for the Brigade. Three was an ideal combination; two could always combine to attack the ideas of one or to poke fun.'

The Sinn Féin Hall in Tipperary was the usual venue for meetings to take place between O'Malley and local officers. Scouts watched the barracks and the movements of military and police while O'Malley instructed the locals on how to wage war to the best of their abilities. O'Malley said that they were never interrupted during these sessions despite many false alarms, and that, 'there was an added intensity in my listeners'.

8

ATTACKS AND BATTLES

A major IRA development in 1920 – the emergence of well-organised attacks on RIC barracks – took on board a spirit of inter-brigade collaboration which saw IRA teams from Limerick, Cork, Clare and Tipperary come together in an effort to undermine British control over large swathes of Munster. Barracks attacks, which happened throughout the country, were also supposed to dishearten or demoralise Irish catholic members of the RIC.

'Men invited to assist in an attack on an enemy post or in an ambush in another area did not hesitate to go,' said Paddy Kinnane. 'This was easily understandable and was not discouraged. During those years there was at least as much, if not more, co-operation between my battalion, the third battalion of the South Tipperary brigade, the sixth battalion of the North Tipperary brigade, and the Doon battalion of the East Limerick brigade, than with the other two battalions of the Mid Tipperary brigade. Our four areas bordered on each other, and comprised a hilly district on the borders of counties Tipperary and Limerick.'

These fights were often unenthusiastically sanctioned by GHQ and were usually led and planned by hugely enthusiastic GHQ fighter-organisers like Ernie O'Malley or Tom Malone (also known by his clandestine political name, Seán Forde). In Tipperary the core team tended to include the cautious Seamus Robinson, the fierce Treacy and the uncontrollable Breen.

Barracks attacks weeded out a lot of minor RIC outposts and *did* undermine the morale of what were seen by the republicans as being 'decent' RIC men. They also used up a lot of IRA bullets and resulted in various insurgent fatalities and injuries.

'In almost all brigades at this time, plans for the attack on a post had first to be sent on to GHQ for approval,' Ernie O'Malley wrote in *Raids and Rallies*. 'That procedure had been occasioned by half-hearted attempts on posts, by unnecessary loss of life, or by the casual misuse of ammunition when attackers preferred to remain at a distance rather than shake a garrison's morale by closer acquaintance. Even in the burning of empty barracks and courthouses, Volunteers had been lost either through carelessness or in the unthinking use of petrol.'

RIC strength was by early 1920 concentrated inside proper barracks, sometimes semi-fortified structures which held large numbers of men and which were less easy to attack. These fortresses might house RIC, Black and Tan, British Army and Intelligence members.

'A pattern to these attacks was soon established,' Joost Augusteijn wrote. 'The local brigade officer, together with the local battalion commandant, and Ernie O'Malley, a GHQ organiser, stood in the centre of its organisation and execution. These men, who were engaged on a full-time basis in Volunteer work, were aided by the most active Volunteers of surrounding battalions. Some local companies were involved in manning blockades on the roads leading to the barracks and in despatch riding. Those involved in the attack took up positions around the barracks, while the main assault was centred on the roof in an attempt to set the barracks alight.'

On 28 April Ballylanders barracks was attacked. Hollyford barracks was besieged on 10 May by Tadgh Dwyer, Robinson and Treacy. The barracks at Kilmallock, Co. Limerick – a British Intelligence hub, and previously a Fenian target, in the Tipperary/ Limerick border area – was burned down on 27 May. In June Drangan barracks, after a long battle involving O'Malley, Breen, Treacy and Robinson, surrendered to the IRA.

Paddy Kinnane led an attack on Drumbane barracks on 18 January 1920. 'The barracks itself was a one-storied building, originally used as a concert and dance hall, which had been taken over by the RIC for use as a barracks. Our original idea was to hold the garrison within the barracks with rifle and shotgun fire, and to force them to surrender by setting fire to the roof. Later we were advised that a more effective way of capturing the barracks would be to blow in the gable end wall ... Selected men from the Upperchurch and Drumbane companies were chosen to take part in the attack, and units from the other companies were put on outpost duty on the roads leading to the village. Our arms consisted principally of shotguns, with a few rifles, and either two or three service rifles.

'When we got to the assembly point near Drumbane, some of the local Volunteers reported that two or three numbers of the RIC garrison were gone out on patrol. A small party of our men ... followed the patrol, captured the two or three RIC men, and held them prisoners while the attack was on.

'We experienced no difficulty in surrounding the barracks, or in placing the charge of gelignite against the gable wall. Everything so far was done without a sound. Our first reverse came with the explosion of the gelignite. It failed to breach or destroy the gable wall, but split it to such an extent that, through the cracked wall, we could see the light inside the barracks. We felt so confident that the gelignite would demolish the wall and make easy our task of capturing the barracks that we had abandoned the idea of setting it on fire, and had no materials with us to put this alternative plan into operation.

'It was, however, then too late for regrets, and after a short exchange of fire and after the RIC had fired several Verey lights [flares] for assistance, it was decided to call off the attack. In addition to the patrol, another RIC man was captured on his way back to the barracks, just before the explosion took place. He was unarmed; we kept him a prisoner until about an hour after the abandonment, when we left him in a farmer's hay barn about a mile from Drumbane.'

In addition to attacking heavily fortified barracks and seeking their destruction, a more common Volunteer pursuit was the burning down of temporarily deserted smaller RIC barracks in less strategically significant towns and villages. This type of low intensity destructiveness, a war of almost casual attrition, was possibly the more usual kind of Volunteer activity at this time

'At Easter of 1920,' said Paul Merrigan, 'the company was engaged in the destruction of two evacuated RIC barracks, one at Glenbane and the other at Lisvernane. Glenbane barracks was burned on Easter Saturday night and on the following night, Easter Sunday, we carried eight tins of petrol over Slievenamuck mountain and did a similar job on Lisvernane barracks. Two weeks later, we put the British Army rifle range at Ballyglass out of action. This was done by burning the lever shed and destroying the lever mechanism with a charge of six sticks of gelignite. The range was never subsequently used by the British military. Activities then became more general and varied. Day-to-day activities including providing guides for Ernie O'Malley, Seán McLoughlin and George Plunkett (who were frequently in the Mount Bruis area), cleaning and oiling the arms, sniping the British military hutments … supplying despatch riders, and the blocking of roads. On the nights of the attacks on Ballylanders and Kilmallock barracks, our company blocked the Tipperary-Kilmallock road and the Lattin-Emly road. Three members of the company: Patrick Power, Con Power and Matt Barlow, travelled to Kilmallock and took part in the attack on the barracks.'

In June Cappawhite Barracks, located within the East Limerick Brigade area, was attacked. 'An attempt was made to set the barracks roof on fire,' said Paddy Kinnane. 'Jim Stapleton, Tom Stapleton and Martin Ryan accompanied me to Cappawhite, and our position was in a house opposite the barracks. Another I remember as being there was Jim O'Gorman of the South Tipperary brigade.

'There was some delay in getting started, and the attack was on for quite a time before the efforts to set the roof on fire showed any signs of being successful. The fire was, in fact, only getting a grip when the attack was called off, as information was received that British reinforcements were on their way from Tipperary town. From Cappawhite we brought a wounded Volunteer to Hollyford, where he received medical assistance. He was wounded in the leg, and he had lost a lot of blood. Dr. Power of Borrisoleigh was sent for and, after attending to him, he conveyed the wounded man safely to Thurles hospital.'

'Tommy Ryan, Jim Kilmartin and I went to Cappawhite bringing with us a bag of mud bombs which had been made from some of the gelignite captured at Soloheadbeg,' said Tadgh Crowe. 'On the same night, the Third Tipperary Brigade was engaged in the attack on Drangan barracks and practically all the "Brass Hats" were gone there. Jim O'Gorman from Hollyford and Dinny Lacey were amongst those whom I remember as having been with us to Cappawhite.

'The attack started about midnight and followed the usual pattern of barrack attacks at the time – holding the police in the barracks with rifle and shotgun fire and forcing them to surrender by setting fire to the roof. Jim O'Gorman used a ladder to reach the roof, but try as he would he failed to set it on fire. He made several attempts at it with oil and mud bombs, but without success. After a few hours, it became apparent that the garrison would not surrender and it was decided to break off the attack.

'Dinny Lacey, Seán Stapleton and I remained there until daylight – some time around 4.30 a.m., replying at intervals to the policemen's fire from the barracks. We had one casualty that night, a Volunteer named Tadgh Hogan being wounded. Some of the Donohill Company who were on duty on road blocks had a fight that morning with military from Tipperary who were going to the relief of the barracks.'

The attack on Rearcross barracks in North Tipperary, but just across the border from the South Riding, during July 1920 brought together nearly all of the most celebrated IRA men in

Tipperary. The man who instigated this attack, which occurred on a cold, windy, and rainy night, was the charismatic Ryan Lacken, a maverick spirit eulogised at some length in O'Malley's various writings. O'Malley had great time for unruly mountain rebels who made up their own minds about everything; their warm vibrant temperaments fascinated his cold urban intellect.

'A well-known Volunteer belonging to the First Tipperary Brigade,' said Seán Gaynor, one of that brigade's commandants, 'who had no rank and had of his own accord and without permission from his Brigade Commandant taken part in operations with the south and North Tipperary Brigades, where he came into personal contact with Seán Treacy, Dan Breen and Ernie O'Malley, urged these men to arrange an attack on Rearcross barracks. This Volunteer was Paddy Ryan (Lacken) … Under the command of Ernie O'Malley, then a GHQ organiser in South Tipperary, a strong IRA force composed of men from South and Mid Tipperary and also some elements of fifth and sixth Battalions of the North Tipperary Brigade, were mobilised in the vicinity of Rearcross to attack the barracks in that village. At that period orders from GHQ strictly forbade men from one area carrying out an operation in another area without the prior consent of the officer in charge of the area in which the operation was to take place. In the case of Rearcross, no notification whatever was given to the Brigade Commandant of that area – the First Tipperary Brigade – by O'Malley or anybody else. By an accident, the Vice Commandant of the Fifth Battalion, Patrick Doherty, heard of the impending attack on the night it was to occur. He at once came to Nenagh to report what he had heard to Frank McGrath, his Brigade Commander. McGrath forthwith sent a despatch to either Seán Treacy or O'Malley, ordering the attack to be abandoned ... O'Malley did not proceed with the attack that night ... The attack took place on a Sunday night.'

'The attack on Rearcross Barracks was planned to commence on Saturday night, July 11 1920,' said Paddy Kinnane. 'That night Jim Stapleton, Tom Stapleton, Jack Fahy and myself drove in a horse-and-cart by a back road to Foilduff near Rearcross, where the men were assembling. Amongst those present were Ernie O'Malley, who took charge of the operation, Seamus Robinson, Seán Treacy, Tadgh O'Dwyer and Paddy O'Dwyer and Jim O'Gorman of Hollyford.

'Later that night, when it was made known that the attack was postponed until Sunday night, the four of us who had travelled together returned home again, leaving behind our Lee Enfield rifles and a pump and hose which we had taken with us. The following night ... we collected our rifles but when the final details for the attack were settled we had no use for them as we were posted to Flannery's shop. Flannery's shop was situated next door to the barracks. Both were long, two-storied stone buildings, under the same roof, separated only by a single dividing wall. Flannery's carried on, in addition to a bar, grocery and general hardware shop, a small hotel business.

'As I had stayed there, I was familiar with the layout of the house: that was why I was posted with the party who took it over. The barracks was divided into three portions by two internal stone walls, and this feature was to have a big bearing on the final outcome of the engagement ... I would say that the strength of the garrison in the barracks would approximate to about eighteen or twenty men.

'Stapleton, Fahy, O'Gorman and myself entered Flannery's house through a low back window. It was then near midnight, and the people of the house had retired to bed. We roused them and, when we told them what we were about to do, they accepted the position cheerfully enough ... O'Malley was in and out of the house several times during the night.

'In the top room next to the barracks we filled a barrel with paraffin oil, of which there was an ample supply on the premises, as Flannery's sold it. O'Gorman then climbed through a trap-door in the ceiling of this room; with a hammer he broke a hole in the slates as near as possible to the barrack roof. Reaching an arm out through this hole, he fired five or six shots rapidly with his revolver through the slates of the barrack roof, to break the slates and also to scare away any RIC men who might be upstairs in that end of the barracks.

'The next step was to bring the pump and the hose into play. With the hose running through the trap-door and through the hole in the roof, Stapleton and I took turns at the pump, pumping the paraffin oil from the barrel on to that section of the barrack roof nearest to Flannery's house. O'Gorman soon had that part of the roof burning. So far, I might say, our task in the house was only child's play, as we worked in the knowledge that we were perfectly safe.

'If the police made a sortie out of the barracks to attack us in Flannery's, they would have been met not only by the armed men in the house but also by a volley of fire from a party of riflemen ... A sergeant, who came out by the front door to reconnoiter just as the attack on the roof started, was shot dead by our rifles.'

'Immediately that we had started operations on top, our men posted outside opened up on the barracks with their rifles, to divert the attention of the police from the roof,' wrote O'Malley. 'I held the long hose while O'Gorman pumped away. Spread by cotton waste and paraffin-dripping turf, the blaze fought the wind and rain, but the swirling wind was best able to impose its mastery. I tried to light the fuse of a mud bomb, and cursed when foiled by the lashing rain. There was nothing for it but to get back under cover of Flannery's roof to light a couple of cigarettes for use as torches, and to smear some gelignite to the end of the wet fuses so that they might light. Out on the roof again, and when I reached the chimney I was able to start the fuses from under the shelter of my coat by applying the burning end of a cigarette to the smear of gelignite. Slates began to fly as I flung bomb after bomb, stripping off quickly large areas of the roof within my lobbing range. The wind was in our favour. It blew flames across on either side of the roof ridge, but rain did its best to help the constabulary. Always, it had seemed, in our few hundred years of outside help, as if the elements aided the British Navy, but here the elements had divided their allegiance.'

It was a grim entanglement. A huge amount of ammunition was being used up by the IRA and the RIC were giving as good as they got. In addition to the rain, the air was full of bullets. Jim O'Gorman quipped to O'Malley: 'When you hear a bullet, it's all right.' Paddy Kinnane and Ryan Lacken, in their abject frustration, were cursing vociferously. Kinnane was dancing with excitement. O'Malley said that he was very light on his feet for a man of his size, 'for he was a grand step dancer'.

'The roof was burning for about twenty minutes or half-an-hour,' said Paddy Kinnane, 'before that portion of it over the section of the barracks nearest to Flannery's caved in. The fire did not, as we hoped it would, carry over the dividing wall and ignite the roof over the centre section of the barracks. However, with the aid of the pump and hose, we succeeded in drenching it with plenty of paraffin, which O'Gorman set afire by throwing lighted rags and burning sods of turf on to it. Again, this portion burned until it caved in; but again the dividing wall prevented the fire from igniting the third or end section of the roof.

'It was in this end section of the barracks that the RIC garrison held out. Several times they were called upon to surrender, but their reply was usually an extra heavy volley of fire. The pump and hose failed us. Either the distance was too great for the hose to carry the paraffin, or else the pump had been overworked. We then resorted to throwing bottles of paraffin, stones and burning sods of turf on to the roof. Some small fires started, but burned themselves out without doing much damage.'

'Seán Treacy came up then to see how the barracks was suffering,' reported O'Malley, 'but he found to his consternation that the barracks fire had now attacked the shop and that it was the shop that was in most danger of immediate destruction. There was nothing he or his men could do to help us from their outpost positions, for they could not alter the situation on the roof. We had been dependent on the pump to keep the flames well forward and away from Flannery's, and the pump had now turned traitor.'

'After some hours' fruitless effort I considered that we could do nothing further from Flannery's house,' said Kinnane, 'so I went, with some others, to the yard at the back of the shop. From the cover of a high wall which separated Flannery's yard from the barracks we continued to throw bottles of paraffin and lighted missiles on to the roof, but with little success.

'O'Malley, Seán Treacy and (I think) Dan Breen were then in the yard. They were discussing what our next move should be when a grenade burst in the yard. Everyone present received some kind of a wound or another; fortunately, no one was seriously injured. I only received a slight scratch on a hand, but O'Malley was hit in the back by a splinter. While he was being attended to, scouts reported that enemy reinforcements were approaching Rearcross along a back road. Acting on this report, the decision to call off the attack was made. So ended the fight at Rearcross. The report of reinforcements proved to be unfounded.'

'We were nearly one and a half days trying to take it,' said Dan Breen. 'We ran out of ammunition and petrol and burned the place. They didn't surrender. Coming back from Rearcross after the fight, we were going through Hollyford and the whole column outfit was there, eighty or ninety men. O'Malley and Jim O'Gorman were wounded and we were walking at the rear of the column – Treacy, Ned O'Reilly and I. Going up through the village of Hollyford, all the villagers turned out and said "Up Sinn Féin!" O'Malley turned to us, saying "Oh, Jesus Christ, after fighting for a few days, see what they are calling us, bloody Sinn Féiners!" Treacy was in charge there. Whenever Treacy was present, he was in charge.'

During July 1920 the Solohead Company heard that a military mail lorry preceded by a motor cyclist passed regularly along the Tipperary-Limerick road. 'Seán Treacy decided to ambush it,' said Tadgh Crowe. 'Jim O'Gorman and Michael Fitzgerald called to me after the ambush and told me what happened. The motor cyclist did not pass and the lorry, when it came, was fired on by the main party. This lorry was closely followed by a second lorry of military who dismounted and took part in the fight. After the first volley it was found that the ejectors of the Martini rifles which the main party was using failed to eject the empty cases from the breech, due perhaps to incorrect ammunition being used. There was then no option but to break off the engagement, and Treacy, they said, saved the day, as he kept the soldiers pinned down on the road with rapid fire from his parabellum whilst the main party was withdrawn. Later, we learned that two British soldiers were killed and three wounded and that General Lucas, who had escaped from IRA custody on the previous night, was in the lorry, having been picked up by the military at Pallas.'

One evening during August 1920 an IRA meeting was held in a barn just off the main Cashel-Clonmel road at Rosegreen. Amongst those attending the gathering was Treacy.

'Most of those who attended came on bicycles and left their bicycles against a wall on the main road,' said Jerome Davin. 'Someone, I expect it was someone returning from a horse show which was held that day in Clonmel, seeing the bicycles at the roadside, suspected that there was something on and informed the military in Cashel. Certainly the military must have got information, for a cycle patrol came out and they came straight into the yard and towards the barn. At the time of their arrival the meeting was over and only Seán Treacy, Patrick McGrath of Fethard, myself, and I think, one other who had remained chatting, were there. Seán Treacy was the only one who was armed. The officer called on us to put up our hands. Treacy fired at him and wounded him. Some members of the patrol took cover and opened fire on the barn, but Treacy, from the doorway, kept them pinned down with revolver fire – he was using his favourite weapon, a long parabellum – while we burst down an old nailed up door at the rear. Meanwhile Paddy Ahearne, the local company captain, who was in the vicinity, opened fire on the patrol, and we had then little difficulty in making our getaway from the barn by the rear door. Treacy then decided to go to Purcell's of Glenagat and he told me to report to Dan Breen, Ned O'Reilly and Seán Hogan who were at my sister's (Mrs Looby's) house at Milltownmore. He knew that they would have heard the shooting and he just wanted me to assure them that everything was alright. In addition to the officer, Treacy's fire had also wounded two of the soldiers.'

SPIES, SPYING, AND FELLOW TRAVELLERS

Know yourself and your adversary and you will be able to fight a hundred battles without a single disaster. Nothing gives more help to combatant forces than correct information.

Che Guevara

Two of the many things which had conspired to defeat the Fenians were spies within their own ranks and their lack of good intelligence – or even attentiveness – concerning their enemies. The failures of past Tipperary rebellions were much discussed by the likes of O'Malley and Treacy as they tramped through the hills, locked in a mortal conflict which they were, palpably, winning despite the odds. They were determined, now that they had the bit between their teeth, to construct a revolutionary army which would know what its enemy was up to, and an army about which the British would know as little as possible.

In order to move their revolution forward, the IRA created a complex matrix of spies, intelligence officers, despatch carriers, and engaged fellow travellers who gave direction to their fight. An alternative realm of deception and carefulness was created which made the British situation quite a hopeless one. No procedure which involved the state interfacing with the catholic nationalist majority was entirely secure.

On the other hand, IRA Volunteers were almost fixatedly on the lookout for spies in their towns or in their ranks. By the end of the Tan War, traitors found within the IRA could normally expect almost summary execution.

In Tipperary, then an insular and clannish county, visitors from the outside world were examined carefully under the IRA's microscope.

Tommy Ryan from the Third Tipperary Brigade presided at the trial of three spies early in the conflict, 'when the manner of dealing with spies had not been formally established'. The evidence against the three was not conclusive. 'They were people of the itinerant class,' Ryan said, 'and the way we dealt with them was to take them by the ear about twenty miles out of the area where they were left, with the warning that, if they appeared again in the area, they would be shot at sight.'

Advantage was taken of the social conventions of the era. Women were supposed to behave like ladies; revolutionary politics wasn't deemed ladylike in respectable circles. Therefore Cumann na mBan women were entrusted with courier work. Middle class young men were considered to be much too respectable to be IRA men. As trusted members of polite society they could do unique and discreet intelligence work.

Dick Dalton, who ended up in Seán Hogan's Flying Column, was a Clonmel Volunteer. Dalton's father was a corn and timber merchant employing over fifteen men. Dalton was called on when the IRA suspected that there was a British intelligence officer in town, staying at a hotel owned by a member of his family.

'Towards the end of 1919 or early 1920 a man who went by the name of Beston – Beston may have been his right name for all I know – came to Clonmel,' said Dalton, 'and resided for some time at the Central Hotel, which was then owned by a Miss Corbett who was a relative of my mother. From his appearance Beston appeared to be an American or a returned American. [A "returned Yank" was an Irish person who'd lived for many years in the States.] Nobody that we knew knew anything about him. He did not seem to have any occupation. It was noticed that he was keen to become associated with members of the Volunteers and, as we suspected his *bona fides*, it was decided to raid his room in the hotel during his absence and to examine his luggage and papers. Six of us … were detailed to carry out the raid.

'My position was just inside the hall door of the hotel, and my instructions were to let in anyone who came along but not to permit anyone to leave. Tommy Smith had a position further in the hotel on the ground floor, while the other four went upstairs to Beston's room to carry out the search. We were all armed with revolvers.

'Everything went smoothly and after I had permitted about ten or twelve persons to enter I must have got a bit careless. A young man came in through the door and, before I realised it, he had caught both my wrists with his hands and forced my hands upwards. My revolver was in my right hand at the time. It was plain to me that he was trying to force me to drop the revolver from my hand. Strive as I might, I could not break his hold on my wrists. Naturally I assumed that he was an RIC man or a Black and Tan in plain clothes, and I tried to force my right hand down so as to cover some part of his body with the revolver and, if all went to all, to shoot him so as to break his grip on my wrists, but the last thing in the world I wanted to do was to fire a shot as there was a patrol of RIC in the street outside. Tommy Smith from his position saw my predicament and came to my assistance. He recognised my assailant as a Volunteer named Willie Dunne from Tipperary town. Dunne, of course, knew nothing about the raid. It was just mere chance that he was in Clonmel that night and came into the hotel. Seeing me with the revolver in my hand he assumed that I was a policeman of some description and thought he would have a go to take it from me. Dunne and I were great friends afterwards.

'To revert to Beston. The search revealed nothing so he was not interfered with further. He left Clonmel immediately after the raid on his room in the hotel.'

Clonmel hotels were not, it seems, terribly secure places for the IRA's enemies. Jack Sharkey, the local IRA Intelligence Officer, was another socially connected young man who could turn his position in society to his advantage. He got a lot of good information from hotel staff.

'Some of these employees,' said Sharkey, 'were members of the company; others were just friendly, but could be relied on. Generally speaking, the "boots" [junior porter] in the hotel was the best man for the job.

'One morning the "boots" in Hearns Hotel called in to me and told me that a British officer had slept in the hotel the night before and that when he (the "boots") brought up shaving water to the room in the morning he saw the officer's attaché case lying open on the bed, and that it contained a Webley revolver. He added that if anything was to be done it must be done quickly, as the officer was leaving at noon.

'I got the number of the room from the "boots" and told him to return to the hotel and to make himself as conspicuous as possible until the officer had left. I then sent for Mr Frank Murphy, who was a nephew of the proprietor of the hotel and who is now [1950s] a solicitor practicing in Clonmel. Mr Murphy was then a member of the company, but very few – even of those in the company – were aware of that fact.

'I explained the position to him, gave him the number of the room and asked him to go to the hotel and, if possible, to get the officer's attaché case and that I would be waiting in a lane just around a corner from the hotel to take it from him. He agreed to have a try.

'Nobody took any notice of the proprietor's nephew entering the hotel and going upstairs. The officer was not in the room at the time. He had gone to the dining room or to the toilet, so Murphy just took the case; down the stairs with him and out around the corner to where I was waiting. I had taken along a large empty attaché case into which Murphy dropped the officer's case, and we both went our various ways. Except for the Webley revolver and six rounds of ammunition, the case contained nothing of value – just a pair of worn pajamas and a shaving kit. I still have the attaché case as a souvenir of those days.'

Sharkey's father owned a successful and well regarded jewellery store on Clonmel's Gladstone Street. When he was twelve his father sent him to Ratcliffe College in England with a view to his going to Oxford and seeking a position in the Indian civil service.

He passed the Oxford entrance exams with honours. When he returned to Clonmel on holidays in 1918, he decided that he didn't want to become a colonial administrator, and that he wanted to throw in his lot with the Volunteer movement.

'The members of the company were practically all young men drawn principally from the shop assistant, tradesmen and workingmen class.' Sharkey said. 'In view, perhaps, of my somewhat different social position – it was then unusual, in Clonmel at any rate, for businessmen's sons to be associated with the Volunteer movement – Halpin [Thomas Halpin, Clonmel Volunteer commanding officer] told me that he considered it would be better for me not to be publicly associated with the company. He said that no one would suspect me of being a Volunteer and that, by keeping more or less under cover, I could possibly be of more assistance to the movement in the years ahead.

'Shortly after I joined the company, but still in 1919, the late Seán Treacy … visited Clonmel. He attended a parade of A/Company which was held in the Sinn Féin Hall in Abbey Street and administered the oath of allegiance to the members of the company. I was present at that parade and took the oath of allegiance from him. From that time onwards we were members of the Irish Republican Army and rarely, if ever, used the term Irish Volunteer.'

It was late in 1919 or early in 1920 that Sharkey was appointed Intelligence Officer of his company: 'It was reported to me that a member of the company was receiving official letters from a British Government department. These letters were delivered to him regularly every Monday morning. It was decided to investigate the matter so, on the following Monday morning, Dick Dalton,

Seán Cooney and myself held up the postman at the Old Bridge, Clonmel, and took all the letters he had from him.

'We examined the letters during the course of the day and, as we found nothing of an incriminating nature, we re-posted the letters that evening in letter boxes around the town. The particular official letter in which we were principally interested was harmless. It had something to do with the pension of a relative of the Volunteer to whom it was addressed.

'The postman returned to the post office and reported the occurrence. As, however, he was in the habit of going to his home to have his breakfast during the time he should be delivering letters, he reported the hold-up as having taken place at a point about a mile further on on his route, so when the RIC went out to investigate, they were conducting their inquiries at the wrong place.'

On 7 April 1920 the Income Tax Offices in Sarsfield Street, Clonmel, were raided by members of Sharkey's company and all the books and documents relating to income tax collection were seized, taken away, and burned. This involuntary tax amnesty was, no doubt, one of the most popular actions ever undertaken by the Clonmel IRA. Since Sharkey was still working undercover, he played a discreet role in this incident.

'Our intelligence service in Clonmel was at this time fairly well organised,' he claimed. 'It was based chiefly on information received through the post office. In this respect invaluable assistance was received from Mr P.J. O'Connell ... He was then personal clerk to the Postmaster in Clonmel. Through him, I made arrangements whereby I received a copy of every telegram which passed through Clonmel Post Office on its way to the RIC ...

The telegraph messenger in Clonmel at the time was a girl named Tynan, a sister of the former Battalion Intelligence Officer. When delivering telegrams to the RIC barracks she had to pass by my father's premises on Gladstone Street so on her way to the barracks she invariably delivered my copy of the telegram to me, so that I often was aware of the contents of the message before the RIC themselves!

'These telegrams were, of course, always in code; but, as I had a copy of the key to the code, it was quite easy to decode them. The codes were changed periodically, about once a month; but as the code for the following period was usually sent to me ... well in advance, I was always in possession of the key in good time. On one occasion I received a copy of a telegram which when decoded read: "The rebels are in possession of our present code. Use this one instead." Then followed the new code to be used!'

When the messages had been decoded they were immediately delivered to the Brigade headquarters by one of a team of despatch riders whom Sharkey had organised. These riders were often members of the Fianna, the youth wing of the IRA. Such boys were not allowed to enter the secret headquarters building or even know exactly where it was located. Instead they took their messages to a cow shed on a farm near Rockwell College. Every day the Brigade quartermaster visited the shed and picked up him mail.

Early in 1921 Sharkey received information from a friendly assistant in the Clonmel post office that the local RIC sent monthly reports by post to the RIC HQ in Dublin. He made arrangements with his friendly post office assistant to be informed the next time that the monthly RIC reports were being posted.

'Everything was in readiness to go ahead with the hold-up,'

Sharkey remembered, 'each man knew his position and exactly what he was to do. But, before proceeding to the post office, I took the precaution of sending one man out to scout around Gladstone Street and the vicinity of the post office.

'This man returned with the news that there was a strong force of RIC and Black and Tans in the vicinity of the post office and that they were more or less hidden in all the shop doorways in Gladstone Street. I then went out to see the position for myself and found things exactly as the scout had reported them. It was perfectly clear that they (the RIC and Black and Tans) had got wind of the proposed hold-up of the Post Office, so I called the job off.

'At 2 a.m. next morning I awoke to loud and repeated knocking at our hall door. At that time I lived with my family in Gladstone Street. I went downstairs, opened the hall door and was immediately confronted by quite a large force of RIC men. They told me that they had come to arrest me and said that I was a member of the IRB. I indignantly replied that I knew nothing good, bad or indifferent about the IRB or anything else either, and protested against being knocked up in such a manner at such an hour.

'One party of the RIC held me in the hall and questioned me, while the remainder of the party searched the house from top to bottom. While the search was going on, those who were questioning me told me to go and get ready to go with them. I made no move to do so, but continued to protest my innocence of having any hand, act or part in IRB or IRA activities.

'At length the search party returned to the hall and reported that they had found nothing which would incriminate me. The RIC man who had done most of the questioning then informed me that I was either the greatest fool or the greatest liar on earth. They took their departure, leaving me behind.

'At the time of this raid I had in the house a Lee Enfield Service rifle which was hidden in a bricked-up chimney place, my short parabellum revolver which was hidden in a niche which I had chiselled out for it in one of the rafters, and a number of important documents which were hidden in the hollow of a marble base of a clock.

'After the Truce I learned from an RIC sergeant who was a clerk in the District Inspector's office at the time my home was raided that a discussion took place in the barracks and that, while some of those present suspected me, others did not, and that Detective Sergeant Stephenson's opinion was that a man with my background would have nothing to do with the IRA.'

When Seán Gaynor took command of the First Tipperary Brigade in Nenagh he found that the level of intelligence gathering being undertaken by his officers was not in anything like the satisfactory condition that things were in further south in the county. He went looking for an entrepreneurial officer who would make root and branch improvements to the Brigade's intelligence operation and found the right man in Austin McCurtain from Nenagh. They discussed what could to be done and concluded that, since their Brigade covered a very spread-out territory, they needed an entirely systematic approach to their problem.

'We regarded it as imperative,' Gaynor recalled, 'that we should have a day-to-day account of all movements of the Crown forces – the police out on patrol within the town or village, where the police and military went for drinks or any form of recreation, how they obtained supplies, how often outlying posts were served by convoys from supply depots, and if any particular member of the British garrison was making himself prominent because of truculent or aggressive behaviour. In addition, it was thought to be most important to have lists compiled of any of the civilian population who might be considered hostile, especially by giving information to the police or military authorities.

'McCurtain carried out the organisation of intelligence himself, and started by appointing an intelligence officer in each battalion and in each company area. He required each company intelligence officer to furnish a weekly report to his battalion intelligence officer, who in turn would condense these reports and submit a report to the brigade intelligence officer ... All intelligence officers were asked to make special efforts to try and make contact with members of the British forces who might be inclined to be friendly, with a view to getting whatever information they were prepared to impart. McCurtain was in direct contact with the Director of Intelligence, Michael Collins ... Generally speaking, very little information was obtained through members of the Crown forces. In Toomevara an RIC man named O'Brien, and another in Cloughjordan called Feeney, did give news of impending raids in their own localities ... In order to facilitate the work of the intelligence staff, systematic raids were made on the mails. Between October 1920 and the Truce scarcely a week passed without such a raid taking place in some part of the brigade area. The battalion Intelligence Officer in Roscrea made seizures at the local railway station very frequently. The mail car between Nenagh and Thurles was so often held up that it was said that the horse would stop on seeing an armed IRA man on the road! Despite all the attention devoted to the searching of the mails, I cannot remember anything of importance having been discovered.'

Liam Hoolan from Nenagh, a significant leader of the North Tipperary IRA, found that RIC men, no matter how benign, were slow about handing over information to their opponents: 'The old RIC men appeared to be anxious to live long enough to draw their pensions and would not take the risk of passing on any useful information. We did receive information through Denis Horgan that when the Auxiliaries arrived in the area they inspected the report books in Nenagh's RIC barracks and wanted to know why the RIC were not able to secure more information about the "Shinners". The older RIC men then decided to sit tight and let the Auxiliaries find out for themselves.'

Bridget McGrath, wife of flying column member Mossy McGrath, ran a photographic equipment business in Clonmel and also used her respectable status as a cover for her activities. She sometimes sent her children to deliver IRA messages and sometimes, when it involved a trip into the countryside, she did it herself: 'I usually carried a camera, and if held up by police or military I was supposed to be out photographing. At the time, in addition to studio work, our business included photographing children at their schools and country people in their houses.'

Dan Breen and Seán Hogan arranged, during the time of the flying columns, a meeting at Mrs McGrath's Clonmel home. She remembered that, at the meeting, they issued an instruction that 'any members of the column with a technical knowledge of driving should seize motor cars for the maintenance of liaison between brigade and battalions. The column members met at my house, 30 Mitchel St. ... During the meeting, to the great surprise of all the IRA men present, Tom Looby, despatch carrier, walked quietly in. Amazement was the order of the moment, as Tom had been arrested near Clogheen on the occasion of the Garrymore ambush, three days previously. Looby had been detained for questioning, but he had succeeded in hiding his despatches under a stone. Subsequently, on release, he retraced his steps to the area, and having again secured the despatches, he delivered them safely at Clonmel. The IRA believed that Looby, having been arrested with despatches, would be held for trial. His release was due to his astute dexterity in the concealment of the despatches.'

The meeting broke up quite late, during the hour leading up to midnight. Two of the men attending succeeded, that very night, in 'commandeering' two vehicles, a small Ford van and a motorbike belonging to an Auxiliary. 'We actually took it in view of the Auxiliaries who were stationed in the Central Hotel, opposite the garage,' Mrs McGrath said, 'some of whom were on the balcony of the hotel at the time.'

Women also got to play more traditional roles, putting themselves at the disposal of the IRA men as cooks, nurses and washers of clothes. Ernie O'Malley liked to paint a *Ryan's Daughter*-style picture from which the IRA men emerged as heroic and rugged individuals cast against a landscape full of craggy mountains where there lived a grateful and staunch citizenry egging the rebels on to still further courageous valour. The women he encountered after the 1920 attack on Drangan barracks seemed to fit this bill perfectly. 'Seamus Robinson, Seán Treacy and I halted near a crossroads by which enemy troops might come from Fethard. We were given cans of milk and thick buttered farrels of cake by women who had remained up all night when they heard the rifle fire in the distance. They were pleased as they brought us out mugs, and disappointed when they found that we could not wait for the tea [a full meal] which they were getting ready.'

Bridget Ryan, who lent her name to the Knocklong rescue's 'greyhound' telegram, had been recruited in 1918 when she got a job in a Thurles office where John McCormack, quartermaster of the Mid Tipperary IRA, also worked. He placed her at the centre of the IRA's courier system in Thurles: 'I received a steady stream of despatches from GHQ for distribution to Volunteer officers in various places. The despatches came to me under cover through the post. They were invariably from Michael Collins, or from another man named Collins who may have been Maurice Collins. Those for local Volunteer officers I generally delivered myself and ones which had to be sent on a distance I either handed over to John McCormack or, at the earliest opportunity, took them to Micksey O'Connell who, in turn, arranged to forward them to their destinations ... Later, Miss Leslie Pierce (later Mrs. Tom Barry of Cork) came to organise other despatch centres and lines of communication and I was associated with her in this work while she was in the Thurles area.'

In addition to forcefully ejecting itinerants from his district, Tommy Ryan sometimes had to deal with more serious allegations of spying. One of these involved Chris 'Kit' Conway, later an iconic figure in Irish socialist republicanism, who died fighting with the Connolly Column* during the Spanish Civil War.

'It was reported to us from a Company Commander of the Galtee Battalion that there was an ex-British soldier named Conway in his area whom he was convinced was a spy,' Ryan recollected. 'I summoned a Battalion Council meeting to inquire into this matter. Evidence regarding this man's movements was sought.

'The Company Commander concerned, while he could produce no concrete proofs of the man's guilt, was adamant in his conviction that the man was a spy. In this predicament I put it to the Company Commander, in view of his rooted conviction, as to whether he would accept responsibility for taking the life of Conway, but he would not accept this, although he still adhered to his belief that Conway was a spy.

'The matter was left standing for the moment but I was not too happy about my decision in the matter, and so I arranged to meet Conway and investigate further. I found out from him that he had deserted from a number of regiments in the British Army during the war, not because he was afraid to fight but because he felt unwilling to fight for England, though he had been driven by economic pressure to join the British Army in the first place. He claimed a pride in being an Irishman and stated that it was his ambition to fight for Ireland. I kept him under observation from that time until the [flying] Column was formed.

'Some time after that, I invited Conway to take part in an attack on the RIC Barracks at Ballyporeen. He was posted in the most dangerous position during the attack where we kept him under observation, with a view to shooting him at once if he showed any sign of treachery in his behaviour. Instead, to our surprise, he showed himself fearless and determined in the course of the attack, and demonstrated to those of us who watched him how a man should behave under fire.

'From that night onwards, he became the white-haired boy and was taken into the Column without having taken the Volunteer oath. He remained with the Column through all its activities until the Truce and was our principal instructor in drill and musketry, being an expert on these subjects through his British Army training.

'Conway was fearless and a natural born fighter. I often thought in the subsequent years that, had the circumstances afforded him the opportunity, he might have become a famous leader like Tom Barry, for instance. During the Spanish Civil War, he was killed while fighting with the Irish Brigade.

'He had a very varied career, having been in the National Army for a time from 1922. When he went to Spain with the Irish Brigade, he assumed the name of Tommy Ryan – that is, my name – and when he became a casualty it was under this name.'

Tipperary So Far Away – The Death of Seán Treacy

> They dug a grave and in it they laid
> The bones of Seán Treacy so brave
> He will never more roam
> Through his own native home.
> Tipperary so far away.

Two days before his death Seán Treacy spoke with Dan Breen, his closest pal, for the last time. Their final conversation was on 12 October 1920 when, in the aftermath of the ferocious Fernside battle, the grievously injured Breen was being covertly stretchered into a convalescent home adjacent to Dublin's Mater Hospital. The people looking after Breen at this anxious time were key players in Michael Collins' Squad such as Joe Leonard and Dick McKee. After Fernside, the considerable muscle of the Squad worked night and day to protect and save both Treacy and Breen.

On the night of 11 October they had been cornered in Fernside, a middle-class house in Dublin's Drumcondra suburb belonging to Professor Carolan from the nearby teacher training college. The elderly Carolan was, that night, effectively pushed up against a wall and shot by British soldiers. Desmond Ryan quoted a British officer as saying that five British soldiers were killed during the vicious battle.

Jumping from an upstairs window, Treacy and Breen ran for their lives and got separated in the fields behind Carolan's house. 'They didn't know Treacy was there,' Breen thought. 'They thought it was Lacey was with me … Treacy was with me and neither of us was in good health after being severely wounded. We had been on the move more or less since 1916 … We were just caught in a corner.'

Eamonn O'Duibhir's sister Mrs Duncan lived in Stella Gardens and her home was a safe house regularly used by Collins and the Big Four. 'I have always felt that had Breen and Treacy got to me in Stella Gardens in the week before the battle at Carolan's,' O'Duibhir said, 'the Duncans and I would have got them shelter in that working class district. It is known that they were hard-pressed to get shelter in the city.'

'When we got out through the window,' Breen said, 'we continued out through the back and over the walls down by St Patrick's Training College. I was not wearing boots because I was caught in bed, and I broke my toes. I went on towards Glasnevin after that … The first shot fired wounded my right hand, and then I had to use my left hand. I had many wounds, including leg wounds. At the time I was more or less oblivious to my wounds, but I suffered great pain afterwards.'

When the attackers gained control of Fernside they roughly interrogated, and then shot, Professor Carolan. He died later in hospital, but not before giving his story to the press. Desmond Ryan wrote in *Seán Treacy and the Third Tipperary Brigade*, 'Professor Carolan was removed in a dying condition to a Dublin hospital. He sent for Miss K. Fleming and Miss Dot Fleming before he died and told the whole truth about the conduct of the raiders after the escape of Breen and Treacy. He said that he was ordered to stand with his face to the wall outside the room where Treacy and Breen had slept, and was then shot through the back of the neck. At first, a British Military Inquiry suggested that Carolan had been shot by Breen's and Treacy's bullets. He made this statement not only in the presence of the Misses Fleming, but also to Mr. Joseph Penrose, then on the staff of the *Freeman's Journal*. His account was published in the Dublin daily papers. No official denial was made, and the story, that Treacy and Breen had been responsible, was dropped abruptly.'

Breen ended up in such a wound-induced stupor that he was delirious by the time his friends sneaked him into the convalescent home. Treacy, not so gravely injured, seemed uncharacteristically somber and downcast in the days after the attack. He had escaped shoeless, beat his retreat across stony terrain, and walked that night from Drumcondra to Finglas – then a country area – before finding a safe house. Profoundly worried about what had become of Breen, he was acutely aware that secret service trackers and touts were on his tail. Those who spoke with Treacy during his final days noticed that the remorselessness had gone out of him.

When he and Breen parted at the nursing home he returned to Finglas where he spent the night of 12 October. On the morning of 13 October he was back in the city centre and recklessly moving around openly on a bicycle. Despite the imprecations of various hardened IRA leaders, he behaved in this irresponsible way up until the end. All day he was hounded by shadowy figures tracking his every move. Anxious to get back to Tipperary where he had already set in motion the formation of the flying columns, he couldn't quit Dublin until Breen's situation was totally secure.

He also needed to get to Tipperary because he was due to marry May Quigley ten days later

While Treacy moved around the city, an unrelenting search for him and Breen went on in earnest. Safe houses, the Mater, Beaumont Convalescent Home, Jervis Street Hospital, and the Clarence Hotel were gone over with a fine toothcomb. A Black and Tan Auxiliary Force placed a cordon around the Mater, planted an armoured car in front of the hospital, and systematically searched the building for three hours. Breen saw the Auxiliaries hunt for him from the window of his nursing home room.

Treacy spent that night, surrounded by members of the Squad, at a house in Inchicore. Next morning he was so uncharacteristically tired that he lingered over his breakfast. When he did leave the house he went to Peadar Clancy's Republican Outfitters on Talbot Street where he met up again with Squad members, all of them armed and ready to protect him. He said he had an appointment with Dick McKee, commandant of the Dublin Brigade, at the Outfitters.

At lunchtime he went alone to a safe house on Heytesbury Street where Seamus Robinson's fiancé's family lived. After dining there he headed back towards to the Republican Outfitters. Those who saw him leave Heytesbury Street were worried, sure that he was, at this stage, being shadowed. He went to a pub where he had arranged to pick up both a bike with low handlebars and a waterproof coat.

Back at the Republican Outfitters he again met up with Squad members who were frantically organising protection for Breen.

They pleaded with him to no avail, advising him that he really should be in hiding.

Treacy took to the streets one more time. In front of the Republican Outfitters he picked up the wrong bicycle and, as he tried to mount it, stumbled. By the time he made a second wobbly effort to get on it, and was just a few feet away from the kerb, two plain clothes officers had jumped off a lorry, lunged at him, and knocked him to the ground.

Moving away from the bike, Treacy got out his parabellum and started shooting at a group of men in suits who were now closing in. Two of them started to fire at him at close range. Treacy succeeded in killing two of his attackers before a bullet went into his own head and he fell down on the ground, dead.

The shooting kept up for another five minutes, killing a teenage boy who was passing by. When the bullets stopped flying an IRA man, pretending to be a concerned citizen checking to see if Treacy was alright, removed the contents of his pockets: two fountain pens, a magazine of revolver ammunition, an encoded field message book, and despatches for Tipperary and Limerick.

He didn't find a letter – subsequently leaked to the press – from Eamonn O'Duibhir in which he expressed his qualms about the violence involved in IRA ambushes.

On 16 October Treacy's coffin was brought to Dublin's pro-cathedral, where it lay overnight. On Sunday his remains travelled by train to Limerick Junction where, at 2 p.m., his coffin was draped in the tricolour. A hearse brought him to Solohead church and, on Monday 18 October he was buried at Kilfeacle.

At his graveside Con Moloney from the Third Tipperary Brigade made the oration: 'Seán Treacy is dead. His death is a great blow to us and to Ireland. But his loss must not unnerve us. Rather must it strengthen our resolve to continue on the path he opened for us; to strive for the ideals for which he gave his life, if necessary, to die fighting as Seán did.'

'I solemnly made up my mind that, if I went into the fight which I intended to do, I would in all probability become a casualty.' Tommy Ryan said many years later. 'I thought to myself that, if I must die, I would die bravely as Treacy had done.'

Jerome Davin had a poignant last encounter with Treacy in Tipperary shortly before Fernside. 'It was at my sister's (Mrs Looby's) house that he shaved and dressed before taking his departure. That would, I'd say, be about a week before he was killed. He told me he was going to Dublin but did not say why he was going there. Before leaving Looby's he wrote his name and the date on a sheet of paper and handed it to my sister. She still has it in her scrapbook.'

A week later the news of Treacy's death reached Davin via a telegram from Michael Collins. 'Seamus Robinson asked me to go to Tipperary town to make the funeral arrangements. A large force of British troops were present at Limerick Junction when the train bringing the remains arrived, but I must say that on that particular night they certainly were not aggressive. As a matter of fact, a party of them presented arms as the coffin covered with the tricolor was borne from the train to the hearse. From Limerick Junction to the church at Solohead the route was lined with British troops, but this did not prevent hundreds of people, including many Volunteers, from marching behind the hearse. Next day when the burial took place British troops were again present in and around the cemetery at Kilfeacle, but the only action they took was to seize some bicycles which were left around by their owners. The officer withdrew the military before the grave was filled in and there was no interference with the firing party who fired the three volleys with revolvers ... To my mind Seán Treacy's death was the biggest blow the Third Tipperary Brigade could or did receive.'

'I remember Dinny Lacey and I were in Dublin when Seán Hogan came and told us the sad news,' said Tadgh Crowe. 'That was probably on 15 October, for Seán was killed on 14 October. On the day of his funeral, Lacey and I watched the funeral cortège from a field at Barronstown Cross, near Limerick Junction. We knew that the military had interfered with the funeral arrangements at Solohead Church and we saw another party of military seize the bicycles of some of the mourners. In view of all the enemy activity that was going on, we reluctantly decided that it would be unwise and foolhardy for us to follow the remains to Kilfeacle Cemetery.'

Breen couldn't attend the funeral because he was fighting for his life in Dublin. He never said all that much about how he really felt about Treacy's death. Perhaps that silence was the most eloquent testament of all. The two of them, since early adolescence, had seen and done incredible things. They had lived life to the hilt and paid an awful price for their adventures. 'People were always telling Seán as he left their houses: "Be careful this time, Seán,"' he remembered. 'His reply always was: "The other fellows better be more careful." That meant that he would fight to the end – no matter what the odds. And he did that in Talbot Street the day he was killed.'

'Some days after Seán Treacy's funeral, the Dwyer's homestead at Ballydrehid was raided about midnight by a party of armed and masked men,' said Mossy McGrath, 'and two brothers, Frank and Ned, were taken outside the door and shot dead, bayoneted and beaten to pulp with rifle butts in the presence of their sister, Kate, who tried to save them. She was the local captain of Cumman na mBan. The eldest brother, who was the local Company Captain, escaped, as his parents prevailed on him to hide beneath their bed … The Company Captain had forbidden the Principal of the local school to open on the day of Seán Treacy's funeral – all schools were to be closed as a mark of respect and mourning. All schools, except Ballydrehid, obeyed the order, so the Captain had the children turned back in the morning and no school was held. It was clear that this shooting of the Dwyer brothers was a reprisal, as the Principle of the school was a policeman's wife.'

Inspired by Treacy, Tommy Ryan went on, after a Civil War in which he fought on the Free State side, to enjoy a distinguished professional military career. His eloquent assessment of Treacy's stature is prescient: 'Up to the date of Treacy's death, we pinned our faith in him as the leader in whom we had the utmost confidence. I knew him well and I knew his worth. He was a man who knew precisely what he was doing and why he was doing it, and he radiated that confidence which we all felt in him. It was men like that who were selected for leadership and who carried the confidence of others, particularly so where, as in my case, I felt that I had not sufficient knowledge.

'Losing Treacy was like losing the captain of a football or a hurling team. We were thrown on our own resources. Knowing the critical situation that we faced and feeling, as I did, that almost any day now we would be in a condition of open war, brought my thoughts towards the critical decision, as I have already stated, where I had made up my mind to die in the fight and to die bravely in the best attempt I could make to carry on that fight.'

12

FLYING COLUMNS

The instigation of the Tipperary Flying Columns – a group of uniformed elite men who kept constantly on the move and rarely returned to their homes – was Seán Treacy's parting gift to his old comrades. 'It was Treacy who first advocated setting up flying columns in Co. Tipperary,' Dan Breen told Jim Maher. 'Shortly before his death he told me that he was thinking of returning to Tipperary to form the first Flying Column in the country. But he never got back to do it.'

On 4 October 1920 GHQ issued a memo calling for columns to be established throughout the country: 'At the present time a large number of both our men and officers are on the run in different parts of the country. The most effective way of using these officers and men would seem to be by organising them as Flying Columns. In this way – instead of being compelled to a haphazard and aimless course of action – they would become available as standing troops of a well trained and thoroughly reliable stamp, and their actions would be far more systematic and effective.'

Flying Column commanders were given unambiguous instructions by GHQ:

1) To gain experience for himself and his men by planning and

then carrying out simple actual operations as outlined in operation orders Nos 1 to 7.

2) By harassing smaller and quieter military and police stations.

3) By interrupting and pillaging stores belonging to the enemy.

4) By interrupting all communication.

5) By covering towns threatened by reprisal parties.

According to Joost Augusteijn: 'The operational orders referred to in point one relate to attacks on buildings; disarming police patrols, guards and escorts and the interruption of their despatches; cutting lines of communication of police and military posts; responding to reprisal parties; and shooting all Black and Tans and the most "vicious" RIC men.'

'Almost immediately following Treacy's death the columns were formed,' said Tommy Ryan, 'and the whole of the best fighting men were concentrated in the operations and activities of these special units. The activities of the Brigade staff from then on became almost purely administrative, giving support to the columns by intelligence and communication services. From the time the columns began Robinson remained in and about the Brigade Headquarters at Rosegreen, taking no active part in the work of the columns and so was not regarded by the men of the columns as having any effective control of them.'

Tipperary No. 1 Flying Column was set up during September/ October 1920, with Dinny Lacey – the coming man – in command. There were approximately seventy men in the unit. Lacey was popularly perceived as being the one to take Treacy's place on the ground, and on the frontline. He shared Treacy's pluck, fearlessness, and commitment.

Tadgh Crowe remembered attending the very first meeting of the column during September 1920 at Barlow's of Shrough. Amongst the sixteen or so men in attendance were Seán Hogan, Lacey, Tom Bellew, Martin 'Sparky' Breen, Brian Shanahan, Packy Ryan, and Matt Barlow. These were the best IRA men available on the ground in South Tipperary. Lacey was appointed as temporary O/C pending the election of a leader.

This troop of notable fighters moved into the Glen of Aherlow where a period of training was undertaken. The republican ideal which informed the Column's approach to billeting hypothesised a sympathetic and hospitable populace. When reality clashed with this ideal, the column foraged as best they could.

Flying columns sometimes billeted themselves in friendly safe houses and, just as often, slept under the stars. Tommy Ryan had to billet his men in a house where the family was deeply unsympathetic to 'the cause'. 'They were uppish kind of people,' he said, 'particularly the woman of the house, who rather resented the appearance of Volunteers or any national elements in the locality. We had very little choice and, reflecting on the matter, I decided that these people with their lack of national feeling would be well known to the enemy and that, therefore, it would be the safest place to stay.

'With every expectation of active opposition, particularly from the woman of the house, I decided we would disregard and commandeer the accommodation for the night, I knocked at the hall door, and finding the family in bed, we informed them that we wanted beds for our men for the night. The family had to leave their beds to make room for us. To my surprise, they received us very hospitably. We spent a comfortable night there.'

Ernie O'Malley was characteristically upbeat about the column/ inhabitant relationship. 'In general, the local IRA companies made or marred the morale of the people,' he wrote, 'If the officers were keen and daring, if organisation was good, if the flying columns had been established, and if the people had become accustomed to seeing our men bearing arms openly, the resistance was stiffened. When the fighting took place, the people entered into the spirit of the fight even if they were not republican, their emotions were stirred, and the little spark of nationality which is borne by everyone who lives in Ireland was fanned and given expression to in one of many ways.'

'It took a while for the people amongst whom we billeted to become accustomed to having armed men training and wandering around in their midst,' said Tadgh Crowe, more prosaically. 'However, when the first shock or surprise wore off, they welcomed us and catered for us with a will.'

It wasn't only the local people who had to get used to uniformed columns roaming through their territory. Seán Fitzpatrick, adjutant of the column, encountered a mysterious nocturnal intruder. 'It was the job of the local company captains to provide scouts for the night, to guard against surprise. As it happened, they were very much on the alert, but Lacey would not be content until he had personally inspected the covered outposts. It was my job to accompany him on his rounds. On this occasion, everything was just as it should be. The night was pitch dark, and we were making our way to our own billet when we were startled on hearing stealthy movements ahead of us, near Alleen crossroads. We dropped flat on the grass margin beside the road, our guns ready for emergencies, and waited in suspense as the movements became more audible. Lacey cried, "Halt" and again "Halt. Hands up" as the seeming sound of footsteps came nearer. Taking no chances and his final shout of "Halt or I'll shoot" passing unheeded, Lacey fired. The noise ceased. We then crept forward on hands and knees, only to discover that a poor old ass, which had been grazing by the roadside, had been shot! Lacey was very sorry but when, in his hearing, I mentioned the incident to the boys, Dinny, in his annoyance, retorted, "Why didn't the bugger hee-haw or put his hands up!"'

'At Grantstown we were joined by a party of nine men from the Third Battalion which included Ned O'Reilly, Jim O'Gorman and my old friend from Soloheadbeg, Paddy O'Dwyer,' said Tadgh Dwyer. 'A meeting of the Column to elect a permanent column leader was held at Grantstown. Seamus Robinson, the Brigade O/C, presided and there were two proposals – Dinny Lacey and Ned O'Reilly. Lacey was elected with the support of the Fourth Battalion men.'

Tadgh Crowe witnessed the column's first engagement on 28 October 1920. 'About 9 a.m. that morning we prepared and occupied a position to ambush a tender of Black and Tans from Golden, but a lorry conveying about twenty soldiers to the rifle range in Tipperary arrived and we ambushed that instead. My recollection is that the lorry slowed up and then stopped before it came into the ambush position proper, with the result that some of our men had to crawl behind the wall to get a position nearer to the lorry.

'Meanwhile, the soldiers were dismounting and taking cover and we had lost the element of surprise. The military officer in charge of the party either wore armour or bore a charmed life. He was firing with revolvers from the bonnet of the lorry and Jim O'Gorman lobbed the only grenade we possessed over the wall and quite close to the lorry, but it failed to explode. Ned O'Reilly and O'Gorman – both crack shots – fired at him from the road but, as far as I could see, without effect.

'The firing lasted, I would say, for eight or ten minutes. One of our men, Michael Fitzpatrick, received a serious wound in his thigh and had to be helped away. He was our only casualty. Lacey then decided to break off the engagement. As the ambush position was on the main Cashel-Tipperary road there was a grave danger of further enemy forces arriving, and the Column, with the exception of two men who were assisting Michael Fitzpatrick, withdrew.'

The first serious operation in which Paul Merrigan engaged was at Lisnagaul on 13 November 1920. 'I was not then a member of the Column, but, on the previous night, eight of us from the Mount Bruis company billeted with the Column near Lisnagaul. We had been selected beforehand to assist in the ambush. It was also the second or third attempt by the Column to ambush this particular party of RIC and Black and Tans on their way to Bansha.

'The position was at a bend in the road about three miles from Bansha and about the same distance from the village of Churchroad. We occupied it at about 9 a.m. My position was with the main party, and I was armed with a service rifle. About 3 p.m., a scout signalled the approach of the police party. As the tender on which they were travelling came into position, there were several shouts of "halt", but as I saw it the driver appeared to put on speed. Lacey blew a single blast on his whistle, which was the signal to open fire. The driver was killed in the first volley, and the tender hit the ditch, but it had also cleared, or partly cleared, the bend of the road. Those of the police who were not killed in the first volley got cover under the tender, and replied to our fire. The firing continued, I would say, for about eight or ten minutes, until the police shouted that they were surrendering. The firing ceased, and four policemen who surrendered were all wounded … When we got out on the road, we found three others dead. One policeman had escaped, and succeeded in getting away. The arms, which we collected as a result of this ambush, were ten rifles (police carbine type), seven revolvers, all stamped 'RIC', some slings of ammunition, a box of ammunition and some grenades which were on the tender. Finally, the tender itself was set on fire after the dead bodies of the police had been removed from it.

'As a reprisal, the British wrecked and burned a number of business houses in Tipperary town, including P.J. Moloney's, Hayes's in Main Street and The Irish House. They also burned down the house of a man named John Bourke who lived near the ambush site. They imposed a curfew from sunset to sunrise in Tipperary town and district, and banned all fairs and markets. My own house was amongst those raided, and I then went on the run.'

Tommy Ryan recalled that the No. 2 Column had been established late in 1920 as a breakaway from the Lacey Column, because there were too many men in Lacey's unit – but he reckoned that nothing much happened with them until Dan Breen came into their area and gave them a shot in the arm. They knew, or rather they felt, that Breen's arrival meant that something was about to happen, that they were about to take some action, Breen's attitude being, 'It's time something happened around here'.

'We felt,' Ryan maintained, 'that his presence in the area meant that there was going to be action and we were all delighted at the prospect and to have Breen with us … On the evening of his first visit Breen came to the house of a family named Fitzgerald, about half a mile from my home. Hogan appointed me as chief scout as I knew the area well. We set off on our first march from Prendergast's to Fitzgerald's. Breen had joined us at Prendergast's and marched with us to Fitzgerald's but this was our first march openly as an armed body. We were welcomed at Fitzgerald's, who got a supper ready for us … We had scarcely sat down to supper when [Mossie] McGrath rushed in to warn us that the military were coming across the fields in our direction. Breen jumped to his feet, quenched all the lights in the house, and called on me to lead him, as I would know the country better than any of the rest. I led the Column men through a gorse field at the back of the house in the opposite direction to which we had learned that the troops were coming, over to a byroad and then down a boreen across the Tonogue river. Having reached this point, I felt I had them quite safe.'

The ailing Breen devoted his greatly diminished energies to bolstering Hogan's column but he was now very much in demand in the Dublin arena where the war was being fought out in a tooth-and-nail style.

'Dan Breen came from Brigade HQ to get the column in shape for the work ahead …' Mossie McGrath confirmed. 'There being strong military centres in Cahir and Clonmel, posting of scouts was carefully observed. The posting of scouts had a twofold object – it was a course of training in military precaution work, and every member of the column received his turn at scout inspection work. Thus, members became familiar with precautionary tactics that proved beneficial later during active Column operations ... Many men were willing to join but arms were scarce and, further, a very large column would not be feasible. In this way many young courageous Volunteers who would willingly fight under the leadership of Dan and Seán, had to be content with company work.'

'The strength of the Column was approximately twenty men,' Paddy Kinnane from Mid Tipperary recalled, 'but this number varied from time to time, and there were periods when we broke up into small parties of four or five, so as to ease the problem of billeting and to avoid large-scale rounding-up operations by British forces. All regular members of the Column were armed with rifles; in addition, some had revolvers.'

On 9 November Kinnane and the column, supported by men from the Third Tipperary Brigade, established an ambush position at Ross on a byroad some fifty yards away from, and overlooking, the main Thurles-Nenagh road.

'We had no time to erect a barricade on the main road when a lorry of troops, going in the direction of Thurles, came along,' said Kinnane. 'The driver was hit in our first volley, and the lorry ran up against the ditch, but did not overturn; later events proved that it was not badly damaged. After an exchange of fire for ten to fifteen minutes and with the spare driver at the wheel, the British troops got the lorry under control and drove away.

'There were several ambushes on that same road. It is what we call a valley road, running through the hills, and even one local man could snipe safely from the hillsides at lorries or convoys passing along the road below. I remember another occasion when Thomas Kirwan of Borrisoleigh, Jim Stapleton, Seán Dunne, Tommy Gleeson and myself opened fire from the hillside there at long range on a party of troops who had come out by lorry to fill in a trench in the road.

'The troops took cover, and we sniped at them for at least two or three hours while the troops replied with rapid and heavy fire. Meanwhile, other lorries of troops were rushed out from Templemore, Thurles and Nenagh, until there were at least 500 troops in the vicinity. They deployed out and up both sides of the mountain, took cover, and brought two or three machine guns into action. Continuing to snipe, we gradually withdrew up the mountain side.

'The British troops were apparently under the impression that we were present in strength, for they displayed the utmost caution and were not inclined to move from their cover. Eventually we withdrew altogether, and crossed the mountain towards Upperchurch, leaving them raking the mountainside with fire. Later we were told that a number of British soldiers had been wounded in that engagement.'

'During our time with Hogan's Column there was very little active engagement with the enemy,' Willie Myles said, giving voice to a common complaint about the No. 2 Column. 'At various times plans were made to carry out attacks or ambushes but always something turned up to upset the arrangements. In some cases we were in position awaiting an enemy patrol but they failed to turn up and, in other cases, our plans were upset by enemy activity in the neighbourhood or something of the kind. By far the most active Column in South Tipperary was that of Denis Lacey.'

Tommy Ryan had initially been approached by Seamus Robinson about assuming command of the No. 2 Column. The fact that he would not consent to being commander disappointed the men fighting with him; Robinson very much disapproved of the appointment of Seán Hogan as commander, claiming that he thought Hogan too young for the job.

'I had suggested Seán Hogan for this appointment because Hogan had indicated to me that he was willing and even anxious to be appointed as Column Commander … ' claimed Ryan. 'Robinson asked me what was the idea of inviting Hogan to take command of the battalion and the Column. I told him that I felt that Hogan was more capable than I of carrying out the duties of such an appointment.

'As I said already, up to then I had had no real active service whereas Seán Hogan, though he was only a boy at the time, had gained a certain fame through his connection with the Soloheadbeg raid and his rescue by Treacy and the others at Knocklong. In fact, his name had become a household word in Tipperary by that time, where songs commemorating the Knocklong rescue were sung.

'He lived at the opposite side of the Galtee mountains but, as his name was so well known, I felt he would be acceptable to the Battalion as its commanding officer. I put this argument before Seamus Robinson. I had known Hogan before this, as I had looked after him when he had stayed at my place for some time following the Knocklong rescue. At this period he held no appointment, but was merely a staff officer going around and having no other work to do. He visited my Battalion area pretty often because he was at that time paying attentions to a girl in that area, whom he afterwards married.

'He knew that my time was very largely occupied in attending fairs and markets. He had put it up to me to nominate him for the Battalion and Column appointment as, he suggested, he had more time and was better able to look after these things than I was.

'Robinson, however, knew Hogan rather better than I did, and his remarks to me on this occasion showed his wisdom. He said, "If you insist in handing over the Battalion to Hogan, you will regret it." I could not see any reason why I should ever regret such a thing at the time, and so Hogan was appointed … He pointed out that not only would he be able to give his full time to this work but that he proposed to bring Jack Nagle of Knockgraffon over … to assist him in the work.'

Training of the No. 2 Column – whose members grew ever more disgruntled with Hogan's hesitant leadership – was undertaken by, amongst others, Hogan and Kit Conway. Dick Dalton said that the Column members had already provided themselves with, 'good strong boots, leggings and suitable warm hardwearing clothing at our own expense.'

'Under cover of darkness,' Dalton said, 'we were brought by a guide named Laurence Hallinan a distance of about four miles across the hills to Derrinlaur where the rest of the Column with Dan Breen and Seán Hogan were in billets.

'Next day the whole Column, which was now about twenty-five strong, with Seán Hogan as Column leader, marched across the hills to Glenpatrick, which is about halfway between Clonmel and Carrick-on-Suir. Here we took possession of a big vacant residential house which was formerly the residence of a solicitor named Higgins. Here we remained for seven or eight days, and I understand that the reason for our prolonged stay here was that Dan Breen was still suffering from the effects of the wounds he received at Professor Carolan's house in Drumcondra, Dublin, and was in need of rest. During our stay at Glenpatrick, food, with the exception of fresh meat, was sent out by the Volunteers in Clonmel. To provide fresh meat we caught and killed a few sheep, first a mountainy sheep and then one from the pasture fields nearby. When these sheep were missed the owners took the precaution of removing all their sheep from the nearby fields. It must, however, be emphasised that the farmers and others who lived around this wild desolate part of the country had no idea who we were. They must have thought that we were Black and Tans for they could scarcely be expected to appreciate at that time that armed Irish soldiers had suddenly arrived in their midst. While at Glenpatrick Tom Kirwan, who was a member of the Column and who had spent some time in the British Army, acted as drill and musketry instructor.'

In May 1921 Paul Merrigan from the No. 1 Column was engaged in the Comeragh mountains, near Crotty's Lake, in the construction of dugouts which were used to stockpile substantial armaments. 'I understand that the dugouts were required to store arms which it was expected would be landed from a ship near Dungarvan, and that the Column was to proceed to Upper Clonea, about two and a half miles from Dungarvan, when the ship with the arms arrived,' said Merrigan. 'However, there were no developments as regards that part of it, as far as I am aware. We spent about three weeks at that job, billeting all the time in farmers' houses in the Nire Valley. About thirty dugouts were made, and as they were completed, the entrances or openings were covered over with light poles and sods. Lacey was dissatisfied with this part of the job, as he feared they would be a danger to cattle and sheep grazing in the vicinity, so he sent eight of us one night to Kirwan's hardware store in Kilmacthomas to commandeer galvanized iron sheeting. Whilst we were loading the sheeting on a horse and cart in Kirwan's yard, two lorries of Black and Tans arrived in the village. Rightly or wrongly, we assumed that they had got word of the raid and that they would surround the yard, so we left immediately and got back to the Nire Valley without any incident and without the galvanized sheeting.

'We left the Nire Valley towards the end of May, and went to Rathgormack, near Portlaw. This was a beautiful and quiet locality for a rest, and we remained there for three or four days. Most of us were then suffering from a skin ailment which, for a better name, we called the "Republican itch". Dr Murphy came out from Carrick-on-Suir and attended us. Our next move was to the banks of the Suir, and fishermen rowed us across the river to Kilsheelan in County Tipperary.'

'One day,' said Seán Fitzpatrick, 'whilst waiting for our confessions to be heard in a friendly farmer's house, the lads were tricking with a .38 revolver, and Sparky Breen, thinking it was unloaded, put the muzzle to the palm of his hand and pulled the trigger. He got a rude awakening, however, when he found that a bullet from the gun had broken a bone in his hand.'

Jack Nagle from the Hogan Column said that, 'About three weeks before the Truce [11 July 1921] the columns were disbanded by order of the Brigade Staff, and the members were sent to their own battalion areas to form active service units. This decision to disband the columns was taken because they were too small and too ill-equipped, particularly as regards supplies of ammunition, to attack the huge convoys in which the enemy was then moving, and it would not have been feasible to muster a column of sufficient strength to deal with those convoys.'

12

BLOODY SUNDAY

> Much of England's hypocrisy consists of acknowledging "past wrongs" while keeping the present ones going.
>
> *Maire Comerford*

Dublin's Bloody Sunday – 21 November 1920 – divided into two parts. In the morning Michael Collins' Squad and associates assassinated twelve alleged members of the Cairo Gang, a British Secret Service crack unit. In the afternoon various British military forces (principally Black and Tans and Auxiliaries) participated in the revenge attack on the teams and spectators attending a Dublin/ Tipperary Gaelic football match at Croke Park. At least twelve people, including Tipperary's corner back Mick Hogan, died as a result of the violence inflicted during the reprisals.

The events of the morning did serious damage to Britain's elite and impressive intelligence organisation in Ireland, causing would-be secret agents to cease living in 'civilian' accommodation (rented rooms or hotels) within the community. After Bloody Sunday they operated out of barracks or out of military bases, making themselves utterly prone to IRA surveillance and to the fatal tittle-tattle of spies (such as David Neligan and Eamon Broy) whom Michael Collins had within the RIC.

The events of the afternoon helped solidify Croke Park's status as a national icon, a cathedral of sport. They were just one more manifestation of the campaign of terror being inflicted on some of the nationalist population by the Black and Tans and the Auxiliaries, agents of an angry empire flailing out in blind rage, unable to cope in a more sophisticated way with the first substantial tear in its imperial fabric. Tipperary was a fulcrum of the ongoing IRA revolt and the arrival in Dublin of the Tipperary senior football team – then, as now, a powerful manifestation of the county's pride and sense of identity – was a natural goad to the British authorities. The fact that the team was full of IRA members and supporters added insult to injury in the abrupt context of the daybreak annihilation of the Cairo Gang.

David Leeson, in his insightful essay, *Death in the afternoon: The Croke Park Massacre, 21 November 1920*, wrote that up until Bloody Sunday, 'there was comparatively little violence in Dublin – so little that Army officers lived outside of barracks, in rented rooms. The IRA's Dublin Brigade was not aggressive. Most insurgent operations in Dublin had been the work of a small elite unit, the Squad, and most of their victims had been members of the unarmed Dublin Metropolitan Police (DMP).'

Between July 1919 and May 1920, the Squad had killed four uniformed constables, six detectives, and a DMP Assistant Commissioner, undermining the city's Detective Division. According to Charles Townsend the rest of the force 'came to a tacit understanding with the IRA that they could perform ordinary (i.e. non-political) duties without fear of attack.'

In the days and weeks leading up to Bloody Sunday the war in Dublin and throughout the country had been noticeably heating up and, by the time the Tipperary team took the train to Dublin on 20 November, emotions on both sides were running very high. On 25 October Terence MacSwiney, Mayor of Cork, died on the seventy-forth day of his hunger strike at London's Brixton Prison. On 1 November Kevin Barry, a student who was tortured during interrogation, was executed. On 16 November the British captured the papers of the IRA's chief of staff, Richard Mulcahy. The commandant and vice commandant of the IRA's Dublin Brigade were captured on the night of 20 November.

The Tipperary team arrived into a Dublin awash with a fever pitch atmosphere of rumour, conspiracy and anger. They were a *very* political bunch of athletes about to undertake a match with significant political undertones and overtones. Proceeds from the planned game were supposed to go to the dependants of dead or imprisoned IRA members. The Tipperary team included IRA activists such as Jim Egan, Mick Hogan, Jackie Brett and Tommy Ryan. Jim Egan from Mullinahone was, like most of his family, active in both Sinn Féin and the IRA. He later died, at the age of 27, fighting on the republican side in the Civil War. Tommy Ryan was 23 at the time. Both Ryan and Egan would be alongside Mick Hogan from Grangemockler when he was gunned down on the field of play at Croke Park.

Hogan was born at Currasilla near Nine Mile House into an old and widely respected Tipperary farming family. He had been elected company commander of the Grangemockler Volunteers the night before the Tipperary team travelled up to Dublin. He was 24 when he died.

'We travelled to Dublin on the previous day, Saturday,' recalled Tommy Ryan. 'The Tipperary team was selected from all over the county in a similar way to which it is today and, as we travelled to Dublin by train, it was not until we reached Ballybrophy that we had our full complement of players ... we were joined by the Kilkenny train which carried four of our players – Mick Hogan, Jerry Shelly, Dick Lanigan and Seán Brett.

'An incident which happened shortly after the train left Ballybrophy station may have given rise to a statement which appeared in the press on the following Monday, that "a band of assassins had come up from Tipperary to carry out the shootings in Dublin on the Sunday". One of the players, Jacky Brett, who was killed later in the fighting, was with a Fr. Delahunty from Kilkenny in one of our carriages. A crowd of soldiers of the Lincolnshire Regiment, who boarded the train, came into their carriage and made some unseemly remarks to Brett and the priest. Brett, resenting these remarks, went for them but he was knocked down and Fr. Delahunty called for assistance. We at this time were engaged in a penny "twenty-five" card game and had not noticed the disturbance. We rushed to the carriage and, when we saw what had happened, we saw red and Jim Ryan and I enjoyed ourselves immensely by playing handball with half-a-dozen of these soldiers. When we finally had them all down for the count, we took two of them up and pitched them out through the carriage window. By this time the whole train was wildly excited, but things calmed down as we travelled along ... we fully expected to be met by military and police and placed under arrest when we reached Kingsbridge [Heuston]. There was no indication of any reception party at Kingsbridge when we arrived there, but we decided nevertheless to scatter ... Hogan and I were, in fact, the only two Volunteer officers on the team and so went to Phil Shanahan's. There we learned of the plans to execute the British Intelligence officers on the following day. It would be nine o'clock on the Saturday night before Bloody Sunday that we were in Phil Shanahan's. We were not told any details of what was being done. We just heard that there was a big job coming off in the morning. While we were at Phil Shanahan's D.P. Walsh [who'd helped organise Breen and Treacy's disappearance after the Fernside fight] came along. Seemingly D.P. had information about the plans for the morning, and he was on a mission to collect arms and ammunition. He asked me to accompany him down to Phil Shanahan's cellar, where there were some revolvers and .45 ammunition contained in porter bottles. D.P. then asked me to accompany him and to carry some of this stuff for him up to Fleming's Hotel in Gardiner Place. The plan we adopted was to walk one on either side of the street on our route up Gardiner Place with the understanding that, should one of us be intercepted or fired at by any enemy agent, the other would be in a position to assist by firing on the attacker ... Having deposited the material at Fleming's Hotel, arriving there without incident, we returned again to Phil Shanahan's that night and I volunteered to take part in the job, whatever it was to be, on the next morning. In between times, we had gone to confession and felt then that we were fully prepared to meet anything that might turn up. Seemingly somebody in Phil Shanahan's that night had got worried about the fact that we had learned that there was a job coming off the next morning, and so there was an atmosphere of hush-hush. We were told that the whole thing had been called off or postponed or something. So we returned to our lodgings and went to bed.'

The next morning members of the Squad and of the Dublin Brigade attacked eight addresses in central and south-central Dublin, killing eleven men, and wounding five more, one of whom died later. 'Most of the dead and wounded were army officers,' wrote David Leeson. 'Some of them were Secret Service agents, but others were just ordinary soldiers. One victim had recently been demobilised, had come to Dublin to purchase horses and was shot by mistake.'

The innocence of this supposed horse trader is disputed but James Doyle, manager of the Gresham Hotel at the time, was one of many who thought that he was a pointless casualty, caught up in the fog of war. 'At about nine o'clock on the morning of Bloody Sunday,' Doyle said, 'I was in bed in my room and awakened by noise. It was a muffled kind of thing like the beating of a carpet. The porter called up to my room afterwards and I asked him what the noise I had heard was. He said that Captain McCormack, who was occupying a room quite close to me, had been shot dead. I got out of bed and entered Captain McCormack's room and I saw that he was then dead. The worker also told me that another man had been shot dead in a room on the next floor over Captain McCormack's. I went to this room also and saw the dead man. His surname was Wilde. I was totally ignorant of what took place or why these men were shot at the time. I questioned the porter and he told me that a number of armed men had entered the hotel and asked to be shown to the rooms occupied by these two men.'

The Gresham's manager said that McCormack had been staying in the hotel since September and had been buying race horses. 'He had booked his passage back to Egypt for December on the Holt Line. Although he had been a veterinary surgeon with the British Army there would appear to have been grave doubt as to his being associated with British intelligence. While he was here I never saw him receiving any guests. He slept well into the afternoon and only got up early when a race meeting was on. When I found him shot in his room, the *Irish Field* was lying beside him. I mentioned to Collins after the Truce that there was a grave doubt as to Captain McCormack being a British Agent. He said that he would make inquiries into the matter, but after this the matter was never referred to again.' Doyle seemed confident that the suspiciously-named Wilde was indeed a spy, having being told by Cardinal Clune* that Wilde was thrown out of Spain because he was well known there to be a British agent.

South of the Liffey, at 22 Lower Mount Street, Collins' assassins found Lieutenant Angliss, the man who'd organised the Dublin Intelligence Section, and killed him as he lay in bed. Another officer sleeping across the corridor from Angliss heard the commotion and began to barricade himself into his bedroom, piling furniture up against the door. He then leaned out of his bedroom window and called for help.

A party of Auxiliaries in plain clothes drove past the beleaguered house at that moment. Noticing the huge commotion that was going on, they sent two of their number back to Beggars Bush barracks for reinforcements before surrounding the building. The IRA men were still trying to break down the barricaded door when they heard the Auxiliaries shooting at them from the street. Two assassins managed to escape but a third, Frank Teeling, was wounded and captured. The fugitives shot their way out through the front of the building, ran down Grattan Street and, according to

Leeson, 'escaped across the Liffey on a commandeered ferryboat.'

Word of the British casualties soon reached the authorities and orders were given to Lieutenant-Colonel Bray at Collinstown barracks. 'There is a football match between a Tipperary team and a Dublin team taking place at Croke Park at 14.45 hours this afternoon. You will surround the ground and picquet [blockade] all exits.' Troops were to guard the streets and railway lines around Croke Park and, 'No picquet should be less than one officer and fifteen men,'

'About a quarter of an hour before the match is over a Special Intelligence Officer will warn by megaphone all people present at the match that they will only leave the ground by the exits,' the instructions stated, 'Anybody attempting to get away elsewhere will be shot.' Every single man present [somewhere between five and ten thousand people attended the game –] was to be stopped and searched.

Alerted the night before to the fact that there was going to be some big move against the British, Tommy Ryan was up early on Sunday morning. As word of the Cairo Gang's decimation reached him, he headed off around town in a vain attempt to assess the situation for himself. 'About eleven o'clock that morning, I got a message from Dan Breen,' he said, 'who was staying somewhere in Phibsboro, to say that he was returning to Tipperary soon and would be glad to have me accompany him. He also said that he thought it would be very inadvisable for me to appear at Croke Park that day. Notwithstanding this appeal, I went to Croke Park to take my place with the Tipperary team on the field.'

As Ryan was making his way towards the venue, so too were the Black and Tans. 'I was going down O'Connell Street,' said

IRA man Seán Kavanagh, 'I was going to a concert at about three o'clock – and I saw a line of Crossley tenders going up O'Connell Street, travelling very fast, all full of Black and Tans. They were on their way to Croke Park.'

Thomas Doyle, in charge of a Croke Park entrance that day, was one of the first to see Black and Tan and Auxiliary members approaching the stadium. 'They were firing,' Doyle told a subsequent inquiry. 'One of them ordered me to open the gate, and threatened to shoot me if I did not. I opened the gate, and as soon as the Black and Tans got in they began firing towards the hill on the other side of the ground.' The sergeant in charge of the Tans testified that, 'I threatened the man in charge and he pulled away the obstacle and let me through. There was a crowd of our own men trying to get through.'

One witness heard a rumour that there were armoured cars massing outside the grounds. 'Almost immediately afterwards the Black and Tans entered at the canal end and began firing.' Another man reported that the Black and Tans 'rushed in as though they were attacking the Germans, and started firing straight away'. The British later issued a statement, in which they claimed that they, 'were fired on by Sinn Féin pickets when they were seen approaching, and returned the fire'. This assertion was eventually discredited.

The shooting lasted only ninety seconds but one hundred and fourteen rounds of rifle ammunition and an unknown quantity of revolver ammunition were fired. Seven spectators were shot dead, four of them shot in the back. Two others bled to death, having been hit in the leg. One victim was shot through the top of the head as he lay down.

'Two men died of heart failure, crushed by the stampeding crowd,' says Leeson. 'Five more people had been fatally wounded. One young boy had been shot through the head, and another had been shot through the body. One man had been shot in the arm, and another had been shot in the back. The last victim was not even on the field when he was hit: he was walking home down Russell Street, away from the park, when a bullet hit him in the leg and fractured his femur.'

'The match was in progress for about ten minutes when an aeroplane flew overhead and fired a Verey light signal … ' said Tommy Ryan. 'The play was concentrating about the Dublin goal. A penalty had been awarded against the Dublin team, and I was about to take the free kick when a burst of machine-gun and rifle fire occurred. The crowd of spectators immediately stampeded. The players also fled from the field in among the sideline spectators except six of us who threw ourselves on the ground where we were. The six of us who remained – Hogan and I and four of the Dublin team – were, I think, all Volunteers. I suppose it was our Volunteer training that prompted us to protect ourselves by lying down rather than rushing around. From where we lay, we could see sparks flying off the railway embankment wall where the bullets struck the wall, and we saw people rolling down the embankment, who presumably were hit. There was general pandemonium at this stage between the firing, people rushing and a general panic amongst the crowd. Two of the players who were lying on the field at this stage got up and made a rush for the paling surrounding the pitch on the Hill Sixty [now Hill 16], which was nearest to them. One by one we followed their example, and it was while Hogan was running from the field to the paling that he got hit by a bullet

… Going across to Hogan, I tried to lift him, but the blood was spurting from a wound in his back and I knew he was very badly injured. He made the exclamation when I lifted him: "Jesus, Mary and Joseph! I am done!" and he died on the spot. My hands and my jersey were covered with his blood. Making a quick survey of the situation, I ran for a spot in the paling. The Auxiliaries had not come in on the playing pitch but were all around the grounds marshalling the people into groups, making them keep their hands up, searching them, while here and there some of them kept firing shots in all directions. As I reached the paling, I saw one "Auxie" loading a round into the breech of his rifle who appeared to be looking in my direction. I dropped to the ground and a youngster near me fell, which I took to be from the shot that was intended for me. So, jumping over the paling, I got into the crowd. At this stage the firing began to die down and I began to think. Realising that I was a wanted man – the police had been looking for me at my home a few days before I left – and that, therefore, I would probably be arrested at least, I cast about for some means of escape. I was the only member of the Tipperary team who wore the national tricolour in my stockings and knickers, and I realised that this fact alone made me conspicuous. I made a dash across Hill Sixty and got out of Croke Park over the wall.'

Ryan made his confused way to a nearby house where he thought that he would be safe. He was only there a few minutes, however, when it was surrounded by Black and Tans or Auxiliaries. 'They forced in the door of the house,' Ryan said. 'An old man who made some remark to them in the hall was knocked down with a blow from the butt of a revolver. One of them, seeing me, said, "There is one of the Tipperary assassins! Take him out and shoot him!" Two of them had bayonets drawn, and I was knocked down and the stockings and knickers ripped off me with the bayonets, leaving me naked. Just then an officer came on the scene and instructed the Auxiliaries to bring me back into Croke Park, where I would be shot with the rest of the team. I believe they would have shot me there and then, were it not for the intervention of the officer who, I think, acted not from motives of mercy, but just that he wanted to be tidy and, instead of having odd shootings here and there, to have them all done together in Croke Park. I was marched along the road, quite naked, and in the course of my move back to Croke Park, I could see people rushing about. They were jumping from the wall out of Croke Park, and one man had become impaled on the spikes of an iron railing. A spike of the railing had penetrated his thigh and, while he was in this predicament, others were using his body to step over the railing. A man who was standing with his girlfriend, with his hands up, taking pity on my nakedness, threw me a coat; but his thanks for this was a blow from the butt of a rifle from one of the Auxiliaries. As I entered the grounds, I saw a priest ministering to the wounded and dying, and a drunken Tan coming up behind him and knocking him flat with the butt of a revolver. The priest was holding aloft the Blessed Sacrament at the time. The people in the grounds had been holding their hands up for about twenty minutes at this time, and numbers were collapsing from the strain. I found myself eventually back at the railway wall inside Croke Park, where I was placed in company with the remainder of the team. I was still in my nakedness as the Auxiliaries had refused to allowed me to take the coat I was offered. The newspapers the following day made reference to a naked player. I was the one they referred to. I and the remainder of the team were lined up against the railway embankment wall, and a firing party stood in front of us. There we remained until all the people in the grounds had been searched. We fully expected to be shot, as the Auxiliaries had promised us, but later a military officer informed us that, if any shooting or resistance took place during the searching of the crowd, he had orders to shoot two of us for every such incident.

'Our clothes, which had been left in the dressing room, were searched for documents or arms. Not finding anything like that, they relieved us of every penny they found in our pockets. That night, as we were penniless, an ex-British army officer, who was in sympathy with us and Ireland's cause, divided £50 amongst the team to enable us to subsist and get home to Tipperary. His name was Jack Kavanagh of Seville Place. When our clothes had been searched by the Auxiliaries and they had found nothing incriminating, we were released and then we scattered ... I stayed that night ... somewhere off Seville Place. There was a raid in the locality that night, and someone about three doors away was taken out and shot by the military or Auxiliary raiding party ... I remained in Dublin over the Monday, returning to Tipperary for Hogan's funeral about Wednesday. I did not go home, however, as the police and military had raided my home looking for me that night, and they raided the place in search of me once, and sometimes twice, a week from then onwards until the Truce. From then on, I became a full-time Volunteer.'

On Monday 22 November the Press Association's correspondent examined the Croke Park pitch and saw the pools of blood where the wounded had fallen and the bloody smudges where the injured had crawled or been dragged away. He counted twenty bullet holes in the railway wall at the north end of the field and saw people searching the pitch for lost property. One searcher found part of a broken thighbone.

'In its official statements, Dublin Castle said that thirty discarded revolvers were picked up off the field. This claim was untrue,' wrote David Leeson.

On the night of Bloody Sunday two important Dublin IRA officers, Dick McKee and Peadar Clancy, were arrested for their alleged part in the morning's assassinations and were shot dead at Dublin Castle while 'trying to escape'. Both McKee and Clancy had been actively involved in the protection of Breen and Treacy in the period between the Fernside fight and Treacy's death. Clancy was the proprietor of the Republican Outfitters store which Treacy was leaving when he was gunned down.

Mick Hogan's remains, accompanied by the Tipperary team, arrived in Clonmel on Wednesday 24 November. Thousands joined the funeral procession to Grangemockler. He was buried in his Tipperary football togs and lowered into his grave by his fellow team members.

Appendices

1

Extract from *Knocknagow or the homes of Tipperary* **by Charles Kickham**

MAT THE THRASHER

The peasant's name was Donovan, but he was universally known as Mat the Thrasher. He excelled in all kinds of work as a farm labourer, and never met his match at wielding a flail. As a consequence, he was in great request among farmers from October to March; and indeed, during all the year round, for Mat could turn a hand almost to anything, from soleing a pair of brogues to roofing and thatching a barn. His superiority as a ploughman was never questioned. As a proof of his skill in this line, we may mention that when Maurice Kearney was about running what in Ireland is called a 'ditch' through the centre of the 'kiln field,' the difficulty presented itself – how to make the fence perfectly straight. And, as a matter of course, Mat Donovan was immediately sent for.

'Now,' said Mat, after looking at the ground, 'where do you want to run it?'

'From this bush,' his employer replied, laying his walking-stick on a whitethorn bush in the fence, 'to the ash-tree at the left-hand side of the gap,' pointing to a tree at the opposite side of the field.

'In a straight line,' he added, looking at Mat as if the problem were worthy to be grappled with even by his genius.

Mat walked away without uttering a word, leaving Mr Kearney and the half-dozen workmen who, leaning on their spades, were waiting the order to begin at the construction of the new ditch, altogether unable to conjecture how he intended to proceed but with unshaken faith in his ultimate success.

Mat walked leisurely back to the 'gurteen' where he had been at work, and was soon seen coming through the gap near the ash-tree with his plough and horses. With one huge hand he leant on the handle of the plough, thereby lifting the irons, so as that they might glide over the ground without cutting through it, till he came to the ash-tree. Facing his horses towards the whitethorn bush at the opposite end of the field, he fixed his eye steadily on that object.

Mr Kearney and the workmen heard his 'Yo-up!' to the horses, and on he came, nearer and nearer, slow but sure, till they could catch the air of the song which he commenced to chant with as great solemnity of look and intonation as if its accurate rendering were a necessary condition of the success of his undertaking. They soon had the benefit even of the words, and as Mat pulled the horses to one side as their breasts touched the whitethorn bush, he continued while he reined them in:

'Oh, had I the lamp of Aladdin.

And had I his geni also.

I'd rather live poor on the mountain,

With coleen dhas cruiteen amo.'

'There it is for you,' he exclaimed, as he folded his arms, after flinging down the reins, 'as straight as the split in a peeler's pole.'

Mr Kearney thrust his thumbs into the arm-holes of his waistcoat, and looked intensely solemn, which was his way of expressing extreme delight. The workmen looked at one another and shook their heads in silent admiration.

Jim Dunn, as he flung his coat against 'the belly of the ditch', declaring in a decided tone, as if there could be no possible question of the fact, 'that nothin' could bate him'. And Tom Maher, after spitting first in one fist and then in the other (if we may be pardoned for chronicling such a proceeding), firmly clutched his spade with both hands, and eyeing his hero from head to foot, devoutly wished 'bad luck to the mother that'd begrudge him her daughter'.

By which Tom merely meant to express in a general way his belief that Mat the Thrasher was good enough for any woman's daughter, and intended no allusion to any particular mother or daughter. But the flush that reddened the honest face of the ploughman, and a certain softening of his grey eyes, told plainly enough that Tom Maher had unconsciously touched a sensitive chord in the heart of big Mat Donovan.

Some readers may, perhaps, require an explanation of Mat's allusion to 'the split in a peeler's poll'. The fact is, that respectable 'force', now known as the Royal Irish Constabulary, have always been noted for the extreme care bestowed by them on the hair of their heads. At the time of which we write, a 'crease' down the back of the head was one of the distinguishing marks of a policeman in country districts where 'swells' were scarce. And to such a pitch of perfection had the 'force' attained in the matter of this crease, that Mat the Thrasher could find nothing in art or nature capable of conveying a just idea of the straightness of the line he had marked out for Maurice Kearney's new ditch but 'the split in a peeler's poll'. We have thought this explanation necessary, lest the split in the poll should be mistaken for a split in the skull, a thing which our good-natured friend never once thought of. The 'new ditch' is to this day the admiration of all beholders.

2

News reports from the *Clonmel Chronicle,* **6 May 1916**

THE CLONMEL ARRESTS

Early on Wednesday morning the Clonmel police made a domiciliary visit and arrested six young men prominently identified with the Sinn Féin movement in the town. Their names are:

John Morrissey (married), builder.
Thomas Halpin, Clerk.
Philip Cunningham, drapers' assistant.
Dominick Mackey, cycle mechanic.
Frank Drohan, coachbuilder.
James Ryan, carpenter.

On Wednesday morning the abovenamed were removed by rail to an unknown destination. Along with them was brought a man named Edward Dwyer (Kate) of Ballagh, Goold's Cross, who had been previously arrested.

ARREST AT ROCKWELL COLLEGE

Cahir, Thursday

An armed party in charge of Sergeant Nolan, of New Inn, visited Rockwell College at seven o'clock this morning and arrested Seamus O'Neill, of Clonmel, who was employed in the College as a teacher of Irish. O'Neill was in bed at the time. He got up and dressed while the party waited in his room, and he was then conveyed to Cahir, and taken thence by rail to Cork.

3

Intelligence documents of the Third Tipperary Brigade, 1919-1923, First published in the *Tipperary Historical Journal*. Furnished to the Journal by Mr Neil Sharkey.

DOCUMENT 1

(A small 3" x 2" pencil-written note with a number 92 stamped on it.)

23/10/21 Int. Dept.

"A" Coy.

To No. 28 Int. Dept.

A Cara

Make a list of the following as soon as possible.

1. Complete list of officers in Mil. Bks. and if possible their records.

2. List of dangerous suspects and records. Send this in immediately as Bn are waiting on it.

DOCUMENT 2

(Letter on squared paper.)

Int. Dept.

"A" Coy Bn 5, 9/1/21

A Cara

Information wanted regarding the whereabouts of a certain man named Connors having the following descriptions:

Height   5 ft 9 ins

Age   21 years

Complexion Black

Curley Hair

Freckled face

Long nose

Wearing grey cap, black coat long trousers.

If said man is found in this area communicate with me immediately and place him under arrest.

Is mise

DOCUMENT 3

(A note on faded lined paper, written in purple pencil.)

A Coy 5th Batn. 3rd April

You will mobilize the following men to be on parade in gymnasium IRA Barrack at eight o'clock Thursday night.

T. Halley Acting O/C

Frank Norton, J. Ryan, Tom Britton, D. Ryan, James Daly, H. Comerford, Tom Daly, L. Delaney, Tim

Shaughnessy, ? Mockler, M. McKenna, T. Cooney (Wood Rd.), J. Grady (Kilmacomna), D. Patteson, Chris Smith, T. Casey, T. Connors, B. Shanahan, J. Byrne, Tom Norris, W. Slattery, Patk. Phelan, J. Farrell (Co-op), P. Farrell and M. Walsh.

DOCUMENT 4

(A 4-page carbon copy of an intelligence note.)

To 28 & 29   21/9/21 Int. Dept.

Int. Dept. "A" Coy.   "A" Coy. Bns.

1. Compile a list of:

(a) Motor Cars   (b) Motor Bikes

(c) Push Bikes   (d) Lorries in Coy area. State make, no. and where kept.

Compile a list of Government officials –

Post Office etc. Compile list of ex RIC in area, also names addresses and occupations of any members of family.

4. Names and addresses of any locals who have joined RIC (State where stationed and character of family).

5. Freemasons in your area.

6. In the event of truce breaking you are to ascertain the following re enemy supplies:

(a) nature of same. (b) mode of conveyance. (c) time and date. (d) route generally taken. (e) Enemy supplies that may be of use to the IRA.

7. Compile a list of the following:

(a) houses frequented by Tans. (b) girls keeping company with Tans.

8. Report any houses the property of loyalists and of good value that could be destroyed in the event of reprisals on our people.

9. Report on all suspicious characters in area and say what you heard about them.

10. Compile a list of girls - giving names and addresses - who frequent Comrades Dance. Let me have same as soon as possible.

11. Watch movements of Ex Sergt. Hanrahan's son and report anything known against him.

DOCUMENT 5

(Letter on squared paper. "Dick" is Dan Breen. The car required was to take an envoy to Dublin in connection with a possible prisoner exchange between the IRA and the British Army.)

To L of S Bn 5
Tipp No. 3 BDE 15/4/21

1. Will expect maps tomorrow.
2. Dick wishes me to say:-
Send word to L/Col. No. 2 where the car is and what is the best time to take it.
3. He also wants you to send him half a dozen films. xxxxx
BDE CMDT.

DOCUMENT 6
(Letter on squared paper.)

Tipp No. 3 BDE 19/4/21

1. Read maps of Ballyporeen and Cahir.
2. 6" maps of Ck on Suir not read.
3. 6" maps will do instead of 25" maps.
Will you order same and forward bill to BDE ADJT.

DOCUMENT 7
(A note written in purple pencil on faded white paper.)

Hd. Qrs
Batt 8 (Rosegreen) 29/8/20
To Qtr. M Batt 4 Clonmel

I didn't get your note re. rifles and ammunition until yesterday as I wasn't at home. I will send them in at the first opportunity. I was down in Newcastle on Monday night also and had your company there out for a patrol. Tis a pity if you don't get a good move on there as there is fine material there. What about having a go at B
there we would give ye a hand – ask Comdt. I think we would succeed quite easily.

Slan leat till I meet you.

XXXXXXXX

DOCUMENT 8

(What appears to be a blue carbon copy of a letter. 'Seán' is Seán Treacy. Seamus Robinson is the Otr. Master and the letter was possibly written to Dan Breen.)

SOUTH TIPP. BRIGADE
22/10/'20
The Commdt.,
South Tipp Bde.

A Cara

You will find enclosed a statement of the accounts of the recent Arms collections. You are already aware of my reasons for resigning. You will note that there is a balance due of £443:11:9. Please let me know who I will make this payable to. A letter to the Head Office on next Thursday will find me.

I hope you are in good form after recent adventures. I need scarcely say how deeply I regret the loss of Seán. I would have been at the funeral but knew nothing about his death until I saw it on the Sunday paper.

Beir buadh agus beannacht:
Mise
The late Acting Bde. Qr. M

DOCUMENT 9

(A purple carbon copy of a typed letter.)

The Commdt. South Tipp. Bde.
SOUTH TIPP. BRIGADE Batt. 2 area 30/8/20
A Cara

I am sending on today two automatics, one Peter the Painter and one Parabellum. I gave these some time ago to the local Company to have them forwarded to Brigade Headquarters but they seemingly misunderstood matters and worse still they seem to have been kept in a hay rick that was heated and they had all rusted considerably so you could have them attended to immediately. There is a box of ammunition also. As regards my recent letter I would like to have a talk with you on the entire matter whenever you are in the locality again, as it is important that we should know what are to be the future movements in this and other localities so that preparations for a general shift of a number of families can be made. The other matter as regards economic reprisals in England ought to be attended to. I refer to the counterfeiting business.

Hope you are all go breagh slan.

Mise,

Do Chara,

The Acting Bde. Qr. Master.

P.S. Please note that the Drangan Company is to be given credit for £50. I turned this amount over to Dan when in the city. I gave also £150 to D.P. on the 17th.

DOCUMENT 10

(A short letter written in pen.)

F. C. No.2

To Lt. Int. Bn. 5

(1) Bearer will give you camera – film still in it but taken. Send out another roll in it and a couple of spare ones. You forgot to leave book after you the other evening, give it to bearer. (2) Will you try to get a green shirt for me – a heavy one if possible. Tell Cooney to send out the boots this evening.

JJ H. O. C. Column

P. S. Hope you will be pleased with the snaps next lot will be better.

DOCUMENT 11

1. You will report the following at once.
2. The exact strength of Yorks and Lancs in Bks.
3. The total strength of RIC at present in Bks.
4. Names of all the Sergeants in RIC Bks.

Is mise

No. 1. I/0 "A" Coy,

4

Diary kept by Seán Treacy in Mountjoy Jail during 1917. First appeared in _Seán Treacy and the Third Tipperary Brigade_ by Desmond Ryan. Ryan noted that it bore no date and was written on prison paper.

AN ATTEMPT TO ACCOUNT FOR A DAY IN MOUNTJOY.

6 a.m. Bell goes. Did not hear it.

6.30 a.m. Warders waken me, unlocking the door. They make a lot of noise doing so as they must give three turns with each of two keys besides drawing the bolt.

7.00 a.m. A few fellows get up. There is little enticement to do so as 'tis rather dark without artificial light.

7.30 a.m. Get up in a terrible hurry. Tidy up cell, etc., if I have time.

7.45 a.m. Lift comes up with breakfast. Another chap and I have to carry it around in C 2. A tray of bread, a tray of twenty two mugs with a pint of porridge in each. Twenty two eggs, tea and milk, a pint and a half respectively for each man. Six of us dine together in No. 27, Eamonn's cell [Eamonn O'Dwyer]: Eamonn, T. O. Maoileain [Tom Malone], MacDonagh [Joseph], Coleman [Richard], and I. Two fellows have to do orderly – wash mugs, plates, clean up, etc., each day. After breakfast, talk, talk. In fact, it requires a strong effort to get away to do anything. We have to collect stirabout mugs and plates for dinner. The time gets used up somehow or other in washing, sweeping out cells – there are two orderlies on duty each day to sweep passages, etc. – talking, making up bed, listening to other people, talking, lounging around, and again talking.

9.45 a.m. Signalling class.10.30 a.m.. Physical drill. Doors open to go to exercise. Visits commence.

11.45 a.m. Irish class under Seamus O'Neill (new arrangement).

Batch of letters come.

12.45 p.m. Dinner. We have to carry that around. More talk. Collect mugs. Wash plates, mugs, etc., tidy up and sweep out cells.

2 p.m. Warders return from dinner. Visits resumed. Knock around and talk. Write sometimes. Exercise if 'tis fine.

4.45 p.m. Tea. Parcels and more letters. Gas lighted. Talk.

6.15 p.m. Military class for an hour or so.

7.15 p.m. Irish class (junior) sometimes. Chatting in cells. Walking around hall. Writing. Dancing. Concert in No. 27.

MacDonagh gives exhibition of dancing on a plate – upsets half-dozen mugs doing so.

9.15 p.m. Rosary.

9.30 p.m. Lock up.

Mass on Sundays at about 7.15. Church door is about ten yards from me.

GLOSSARY

1798. The rebellion which happened in that year was organised by the United Irishmen, a revolutionary organisation which sought to bring together catholics, protestants and dissenters in order to remove English control over Irish affairs. The events of 1798, ironically, resulted in the 1801 Act of Union, which brought Ireland directly under British control. Inspired by the French Revolution, the United Irishmen were led by Theobald Wolfe Tone, Thomas Russell, Henry Joy McCracken and William Drennan. Secret, oath-bound, and dedicated to a republican form of government in a separate and independent Ireland, their rebellion scored significant triumphs in Co. Wexford and was supported, up to a point, by the French government.

Act of Union. See 1798.

Bureau of Military History. For more information see *In Such Deadly Earnest* by Diarmaid Ferriter in *The Dublin Review*, No. 12. Also *Dan Breen and the IRA* by Joe Ambrose.

Casement, Roger. Hanged for his part in the 1916 Rising, Casement was a distinguished human rights activist who in 1903 investigated forced labour in the Belgian Congo. In 1910 he looked into colonial atrocities in Latin America. By 1914 he was in Berlin trying to persuade the German government to support an independent Ireland. He was sent back to Ireland in time for the 1916 Rising in a German U Boat which left him off at Banna Strand, Co. Kerry. He was soon arrested, charged with treason, and hung in Pentonville Prison. It later emerged that his 'Black Diaries', which contained numerous exceptionally explicit homosexual references, had been circulated to those in liberal London society who'd sought a reprieve for him. It is acknowledged that the circulation of the diaries sealed his fate. There was, for decades, a raging controversy concerning the authenticity or otherwise of the diaries, with nationalist apologists blithely claiming that it was inconceivable that a valiant Irish patriotic hero could have entertained such fetid thoughts and such dark desires.

Chartists. A UK movement for political and social reform whose name derived from the People's Charter of 1838, which called for universal suffrage, electoral reform, regular wages to be paid to politicians, and annual elections to parliament..

Citizen Army. See James Connolly.

Clune, Cardinal P.J.. Born in 1864 near Ruan, Co. Clare, Clune enjoyed an impressive career in the Australian catholic church. In 1913 he was made Archbishop of Perth. A dedicated Home Ruler, in WWI he was senior chaplain to the Catholic members of the Australian Imperial Force. In 1916 he visited troops in England and at Ypres. On a visit to Ireland in 1920 he was deeply shocked by the behaviour of the Black and Tans. He attempted to negotiate between the British government and the Sinn Féin leaders; conferring with Lloyd George and members of his cabinet. He commuted between London and Dublin for weeks, conveying the cabinet's terms to the Irish leaders and their replies to Lloyd George. Nothing came of his intercession. In Paris in January 1921, on his way to Rome, Clune stated publicly that he believed Lloyd George 'sincerely yearned for peace' but that, unhappily, members of his government did not share this views; he said that the Sinn Féiners as 'the cream of their race'.

Connolly, James. Born in Edinburgh of Irish parents, worked in a printing works as a child before joining the British Army. Principally stationed around Cork, where he noted how the state treated the people. In 1896 Connolly founded the Irish Socialist Republican Society and a paper –*The Worker's Republic*. After a peripatetic socialist life he settled in Dublin where he helped found the Citizens Army in 1913 to defend striking workers facing police and Employer Federation intimidation. In 1915 Connolly was appointed acting General Secretary of the Irish Transport and General Workers Union. Because of the Citizen Army's strident posturing, the IRB took Connolly into their confidences and told him about the planned 1916 rebellion. Appointed Military Commander of the Republican Forces in Dublin, he was one of the seven signatories to the Proclamation which announced the existence of a progressively-orientated Irish Republic. He was one of the 1916 leaders executed after the Rising. Prior to his death that part of Irish nationalism which was also socialist-minded was miniscule. Ever since his death, republican socialism has been a significant thread in the revolutionary strand. Those influenced by Connolly include disparate figures such as Peadar O'Donnell, Seamus Costello, David Thornley, and Bernadette Devlin.

Connolly Column. Also known as the Irish Brigade, the Connolly Column, founded by Peadar O'Donnell in 1936, were leftist ex-IRA men and socialists who fought on the side of the Spanish Republic in the Spanish Civil War, 1936-1939. Their story is told in Michael O'Riordan's partisan but lively book, *The Connolly Column*. Significant members of the Column included O'Riordan (the diriving force behind the Irish Communist Party), IRA leader Frank Ryan, Kit Conway, and Charlie Donnelly, Conway was killed in action at Jarama in February 1937

Cumann na mBan. The women's revolutionary organisation which worked alongside the IRA. It aimed, by force of arms, to drive the British out of Ireland, to 'advance the cause of Irish liberty', and to 'teach its members first aid, drill, signalling and rifle practice in order to aid the men of Ireland'. Having played an active shooting role in the 1916 Rising, the organisation was led and revived thereafter by Countess Markiewicz, 'the comrade who had no comrade'. She became Minister for Labour in the first Irish government.

Dungannon Clubs. See Bulmer Hobson

Hobson, Bulmer. Socialist and journalist Hobson was a member of the Supreme Council of the IRB. He was, with Denis McCullough, one of the founders in 1904 of the Dungannon Clubs which rejected Home Rule in favour of total Irish independence from Britain. He was not informed of the plans for the 1916 Rising because he no longer enjoyed the confidence of the IRB high command. It was Hobson who, opposed to the coming Rising, told Eoin MacNeill what the IRB were up to. This action lead to MacNeill's countermanding order which threw the conspiracy into disarray. Hobson was kidnapped by the IRB to stop him from spreading news of the countermanding order and he was held capitve by Maurice Collins, who later acted as a conduit for Michael Collins' despatches to the provinces. He played no further part in Irish history, being sidelined into a minor civil service job after independence.

Land League. Aimed to abolish landlordism so that tenant farmers could own the land they worked on. Founded in 1878 and reconstituted in 1879 with Parnell at its helm and Michael Davitt by his side, it set out to bring about a reduction of rents and to transfer ownership of the soil to its occupiers. It fought for these objectives during the Land War of 1880–1882, using rent strikes, boycott, parliamentary clout, and intimidation.

Maxwell, Sir John. A distinguished military career during WW1, which included victory at the Battle of the Marne and spells in charge of the British forces in troublesome Egypt culminated in Maxwell being in military command in Ireland at the time of the 1916 rebellion. His imposition of martial law and his decision to execute the 1916 ringleaders – endorsed by the British government – had a catastrophic effect on the entire British imperial adventure. It was the harsh treatment of the revolutionaries which bought about a degree of support for the emergent IRA, and it was the IRA who first proved that the British Empire could be repelled at gunpoint.

McCan, Pierce. For information on McCan see Deaglán O'Bric's *Pierce McCan, MP* in the 1986 and 1989 *Tipperary Historical Journal.* Also *Dan Breen and the IRA* by Joe Ambrose.

MacDermott, Seán. Also known as Seán Mac Diarmada. One of the leaders of the 1916 Rising and a signatory of the proclomation of the Republic. A member of the Supreme Council of the IRB, he was a national organiser for that organisation and, in that context, travelled the country in the years leading up to 1916. He was one of the principal organisers of the Rising and was executed for his part in it.

Mellows, Liam. Commanded the Western Division of the Volunteers during the 1916 Rising, leading abortive attacks on RIC barracks at Oranmore and Clarinbridge, Co. Galway. Escaping to the United States, he was arrested and detained without trial in New York's Tombs prison. He returned to Ireland to become the IRA's director of supplies during the Tan War with responsiblity for arms purchases. He took the Republican side in the Civil War, stating in the Dail that: 'We do not seek to make this country a materially great country at the expense of its honour in any way whatsoever. We would rather have this country poor and indigent, we would rather have the people of Ireland eking out a poor existence on the soil; as long as they possessed their souls, their minds, and their honour. This fight has been for something more than the fleshpots of Empire.' He was executed by the Free State during the Civil War in 1922.

Parnellism. Charles Stewart Parnell was leader of the Irish Parliamentary Party which sought Home Rule for Ireland. Parnell was one of the most enigmatic and charismatic of Irish leaders, a noted Westminster politician and a wily political operator whose many achievements include the partial reform of the land question in Ireland. He achieved this through his historic alliance with former Fenian Michael Davitt in the Land League. He encouraged the use of boycott as a means of pressurising landlords. Destroyed by a sex scandal of sorts, Parnell died in 1891 and became an idealised iconic figure for the emergent revolutionary generation.

Redmondite. See Parnellism. John Redmond led the Irish Parliamentary Party between 1900 and his death in 1918. In the general election which took place in that year, the Irish Party lost most of its parliamentary seats to Sinn Féin. Tension and animosity existed between Redmondites, men of moderation quite comfortable in the House of Commons, and the Sinn Féiners who supported a broad range of more radical agendas.

Ribbonmen. Mid-nineteenth century secret gangs of rural catholics opposed to the Orange Order. The Ribbonmen were anti-Protestant, anti-British, anti-tithes, and active in land disputes.

Sheehan, Donal. One of three Volunteers who drowned at Ballykissane, Co. Kerry, during a botched 1916 attempt to liaise with the German boat, The *Aud*, which was bringing armaments to Fenit for a proposed Kerry Rising involving Roger Casement and Austin Stack.

The O'Rahilly. Director of Arms for the Irish Volunteers but not a member of the IRB, he was one of those, along with Bulmer Hobson and Eoin MacNeill, who opposed the 1916 Rising on the grounds that it was a hopeless gesture. When he heard about the kidnap of Bulmer Hobson he stormed into Patrick Pearse's study and annouced, brandishing a revolver, that, 'Whoever kidnaps me will have to be a quicker shot!' O'Rahilly was temporarily mollified by Pearse but immediately thereafter drove out of Dublin to undertake an extraordinary overnight car journey, which took him all over the south of Ireland, to pass on word of MacNeill's countermanding order. When the Rising eventually happened he decided to take his place in the GPO along with the other rebels – allegedly saying, 'Well, I've helped to wind up the clock – I might as well hear it strike!' He was, eventually, shot dead by British machine gun fire. He is commemorated, at the spot where he died, by an elegant memorial created by the distinguished contemporary Irish artist Shane Cullen.

Threshing machine. A piece of farm machinery used to separate grain from stalks and husks. By the time of the Tan War most threshing machines would have been steam-driven, having previously been horse-powered. Threshing machines were eventually supplanted by combine harvesters. 'The treshin' was always a major social occasion and a time of hard work on an Irish farm, with the women of the house preparing food and drink for the large retinue of men who would come onto a farm to do the threshing.

Whiteboys. A secret eighteenth century agrarian organisation using violence to defend the rights of tenant farmers. Whiteboy agitation first manifested itself in Limerick in 1761 and quickly spread to counties Tipperary, Cork, and Waterford. Initially they used nonviolent tactics such as the levelling of ditches that closed off common grazing land but eventually they developed a violent reputation.

SOURCES BY CHAPTER

INTRODUCTION

Augusteijn – From Public Defiance to Guerrilla Warfare (Irish Academic Press; Dublin, 1996), Joost Augusteijn

Malone – Blood on the Flag by James Malone. Translated from Irish by Patrick J. Twohig (Tower Books: Cork, 1996)

Ryan – Seán Treacy and the 3rd Tipperary Brigade, Desmond Ryan (Alliance Books; London, 1945)

Statement – Bureau of Military History Statement

THJ – Tipperary Historical Journal

Thomas Ryan – One Man's Flying Column by Thomas Ryan, *Tipperary Historical Journal*, 1991

Kinnane – Paddy Kinnane, *My Part in the War of Independence*, *Tipperary Historical Journal*, 1995

Tadgh Crowe – Tadgh Crowe, *Life with a Flying Column, 1919–1921*, *Tipperary Historical Journal*, 2004

CHAPTER 1

Power, Patrick C., *History of South Tipperary* (Mercier Press; Cork, 1989) [Detailed information on the Young Irelanders in Tipperary]

Michael Murphy, conversation with the author.

Mitford, Nancy, *The Water Beetle* (Hamish Hamilton; London, 1962)

Augusteijn, Joost, *Why was Tipperary so Active in the War of Independence? THJ*, 2006

Clancy, Liam, *Memoirs of an Irish Troubadour* (Virgin Books; London, 2002)

MacManus, M.J., ed., *Thomas Davis and Young Ireland*, (Stationery Office; Dublin, 1945) [Donagh MacDonagh quote]

Moody, T.W., ed., *The Fenian Movement* (Mercier Press; Cork, 1967) [Desmond Ryan quote]

O'Malley, Ernie, *On Another Man's Wound* (Rich & Cowan; London, 1937)

Brown, Malcolm *The Politics of Irish Literature from Thomas Davis to W.B. Yeats* [Young Irelander Ideas]

CHAPTER 2

Moody, T.W., ed., *The Fenian Movement* [Desmond Ryan, Kevin B. Nowlan, and E.R.R. Green quotes]

O'Donnell, Michael, *Michael Doheny Fenian Leader*, a 1986 lecture published on www.fethard.com

Power, *History of South Tipperary* [Detailed information on the Fenians in Tipperary]

Brown, *The Politics of Irish Literature* [Doheny and Stephen's journey across Munster, Fenians ideas, the Irish People, Kickham]

Bourke, Marcus *John O'Leary; A Study in Irish Separatism* (University of Georgia Press; Athens, Georgia, 1967) [O'Leary's speech in Tipperary town when unveiling the Kickham monument]

CHAPTER 3

Nolan, William and McGrath, Thomas, eds, *Tipperary; History and Society* (Geography Publications; Dublin, 1985) [essays *Joseph K. Bracken, G.A.A. Founder, Fenian, and politician* by Nancy Murphy and *County Tipperary; class struggle and national struggle, 1916-1924* by D.R. O'Connor Lysaght]

Ahearn, Michael, *Sketches from a Clonmel Landscape* [Information on Frank Drohan] 2006

Myles, William, *Easter Week in Clonmel*, in *Cluain Meala, 2006*

Clonmel – Easter 1916, in *Cluain Meala* (Clonmel, 1966)

William Myles *Statement*

Dan Breen *Statement*

Ryan [Seán Treacy and 1916, Mick O'Callaghan story, Seán Horan quote, Paddy Ryan quote]

Breen Dan, *My Fight for Irish Freedom,* (Anvil Books; Dublin, 1964)

Dan Breen, *Statement*

Augusteijn [RIC report]

CHAPTER 4

Malone [Brigid Walsh story]

Uinseánn MacEoin, *Survivors*, (Argenta Publications; Dublin, 1980) [Thomas Malone quote]

Kinnane

Tadgh Crowe

Thomas Ryan

Augusteijn [Paddy Ryan "Lacken" quote]

CHAPTER 5

Ryan

Ernie O'Malley, *On Another Man's Wound*

William Myles *Statement*

Thomas Ryan

CHAPTER 6

Ryan [Prison correspondance, Maurice Crowe quote]

Richard Mulcahy, *Chief of Staff, Capuchin Annual,* 1969
Tadgh Crowe

CHAPTER 7

Dan Breen, *Statement*

Jerome Davin, *Statement*

Tadgh Crowe

Ryan [Maurice Crowe quote, Godfrey evidence, Quinn evidence, Knocklong, Ashtown Road]

Seamus Robinson *Statement*

Paddy O'Dwyer *Statement*

Thomas Ryan

Eamonn O'Duibhir *Statement*

Mick Davern *Statement*

Bridget Ryan *Statement*

Malone

Dan Breen *Statement*

Annie Farrington *Statement*

Vinnie Byrne *Statement*

Ernie O'Malley, *On Another Man's Wound*

CHAPTER 8

Augusteijn [barracks attacks]

Kinnane

Ernie O'Malley, *Raids and Rallies*

Paul Merrigan *Statement*

Seán Gaynor *Statement*

Dan Breen *Statement*

Tadgh Crowe

Jerome Davin *Statement*

CHAPTER 9

Thomas Ryan

Richard Dalton *Statement*

Seán Sharkey, *My Role as an Intelligence Officer with the Third Tipperary Brigade (1919–1921), THJ*, 1998

Seán Gaynor *Statement*

Liam Hoolan *Statement*

Bridget McGrath *Statement*

Bridget Ryan *Statement*

CHAPTER 10

Ryan [Fernside, Treacy's final days]

Dan Breen *Statement*

Eamonn O'Duibhir *Statement*

Thomas Ryan

Jerome Davin *Statement*

Tadgh Crowe

Jim Maher, *Dan Breen looks back 50 years from 1967, THJ*, 1998
[Dan Breen quote]

Maurice McGrath *Statement*

CHAPTER 11

Augusteijn [Flying Columns]

Jim Maher, *Dan Breen looks back 50 years from 1967, THJ*, 1998
[Dan Breen quote]

Tadgh Crowe

English, Richard, *The inborn hate of things English : Ernie O'Malley and the Irish Revolution 1916–1923, Past & Present*, 1996

[Ernie O'Malley quote]

Seán Fitzpatrick *Statement*

Tadgh Dwyer *Statement*

Paul Merrigan *Statement*

Maurice McGrath *Statement*

Kinnane

William Myles *Statement*

Patterson, Tony, *Third Tipperary Brigade, Number Two Flying Column, January to June 1921, THJ*, 2006 [Dick Dalton and Jack Nagle quotes]

Andrew Kennedy *Statement*

CHAPTER 12

Leeson, David, *'Death in the afternoon: The Croke Park Massacre', 21 November 1920, Canadian Journal of History*, April, 2003

Thomas Ryan

James Doyle *Statement*

Bibliography

BOOKS

Ahearn, Michael, *Figures from a Clonmel Landscape* (Clonmel, 2006)

Ambrose, Joe, *Dan Breen and the IRA* (Mercier Press; Cork, 2006)

Annacarty/Donohill Cultural and Historical Society, *Annacarty/ Donohill History* (Tipperary, 1997)

Augusteijn, Joost, *From Public Defiance to Guerrilla Warfare* (Irish Academic Press; Dublin, 1996)

Breen, Dan, *My Fight for Irish Freedom* (Anvil Books; Dublin, 1964)

Bourke, Marcus, *John O'Leary; A Study in Irish Separatism* (University of Georgia Press; Athens, Georgia, 1967)

Brown, Malcolm, *The Politics of Irish Literature From Thomas Davis to W.B. Yeats* (Allen and Unwin; London, 1972)

Cluain Meala (Clonmel, 1966)

Comerford, R.V., *Charles J Kickham; A Study of Irish nationalism and literature* (Wolfhound; Dublin, 1979)

Coogan, Tim Pat, *The IRA* (Fontana; London, 1980)

Doheny, Michael, *The Felon's Track* (www.gutenberg.org)

Doherty, Gabriel, Keogh, Dermot, (eds), *1916 – The Long Revolution* (Mercier Press; Cork, 2007)

English, Richard, *Irish Freedom: The History of Nationalism in Ireland* (Pan Macmillan; London, 2006)

—— *Armed Struggle: The History of the IRA* (Pan Macmillan; London, 2003)

—— *Ernie O'Malley: IRA Intellectual* (Oxford University Press; Oxford, 1998)

Garvin, Tom, *Nationalist revolutionaries in Ireland 1858-1928* (Clarendon Press; Oxford, 1987.)

Griffith, Kenneth and O'Grady, Timothy, *Curious Journey; An Oral History of Ireland's Unfinished Revolution* (Hutchinson; London, 1987)

McCarthy, J.M.(ed.), *Limerick's Fighting Story* (*The Kerryman*; Tralee, 1947)

MacEoin, Uinseánn *Survivors* (Argenta Publications; Dublin, 1980)

MacManus, M.J. (ed.), *Thomas Davis and Young Ireland* (Stationery Office; Dublin, 1945)

Moody, T.W. (ed.), *The Fenian Movement* (Mercier Press; Cork, 1967)

Mulcahy, Risteárd, *Richard Mulcahy (1886-1971): A Family Memoir* (Dublin; Aurelian Press, 1999)

Nolan, William, and McGrath, Thomas (eds), *Tipperary; History and Society* (Geography Publications; Dublin, 1985)

Nowlan, Kevin B., (ed.), *The Making of 1916; Studies in the History of the Rising* (Stationery Office; Dublin, 1969)

O'Connor, Ulick, *A Terrible Beauty is Born: The Irish troubles, 1912–1922*, (Hamish Hamilton; London, 1975)

O'Donoghue, Florence, (ed.), *Sworn to be Free – The Complete Book of IRA Jailbreaks 1918–1921* (Anvil Press; Tralee; 1971)

O'Dwyer, Martin, *A Pictorial History of Tipperary 1916-1923* (The Folk Village; Cashel, 2004)

O'Farrell, Padraic, *Who's Who in the Irish War of Independence and Civil War 1916–1923* (Lilliput Press; Dublin, 1997)

——— *The Ernie O'Malley Story* (Mercier Press; Cork, 1983)

O'Leary, John, *Recollections of Fenians and Fenianism* (London, 1896)

O'Malley, Ernie, *On Another Man's Wound* (Rich & Cowan; London, 1937)

——— *Raids and Rallies* (Anvil Books; Dublin, 1982)

——— *The Singing Flame* (Anvil Books; Dublin, 1978)

Power, Patrick C., *History of South Tipperary* (Mercier Press; Cork, 1989)

Ryan, Desmond, *Seán Treacy and the Third Tipperary Brigade* (Alliance Books; London, 1945)

Ryan, Meda, *The Real Chief; The Story of Liam Lynch* (Mercier Press; Cork, 1996)

Shelley, John R, *A Short History of the 3rd Tipperary Brigade* (Tipperary, 1996)

Townsend, Charles, *The British Campaign in Ireland, 1919–1921* (Oxford University Press; Oxford, 1975)

——— *Political Violence in Ireland* (Oxford University Press; Oxford, 1983)

Williams, T. Desmond, *The Irish Struggle, 1916–1926* (Routledge Kegan Paul; London, 1966)

——— *Secret Societies in Ireland* (Gill & Macmillan; Dublin; 1973)

ARTICLES

Tipperary Historical Journal 1986
Ó Bric, Deaglán, *Pierce McCan, MP*

Tipperary Historical Journal 1989
Ó Bric, Deaglán, *Pierce McCan, MP Part 2*

Tipperary Historical Journal 1991
Ó Duibhir, Eamonn, *The Tipperary Volunteers in 1916: A Personal Account 75 Years On*
Ryan, Thomas, *One Man's Flying Column*

Tipperary Historical Journal 1992
Ryan, Thomas, *One Man's Flying Column; Part 2*

Tipperary Historical Journal 1993
Gaynor, Séan, *With Tipperary No. 1 Brigade in North Tipperary 1917–1921*
Ryan, Thomas, *One Man's Flying Column: Part 3*

Tipperary Historical Journal 1994
Gaynor, Séan, *With the Tipperary No. 1 Brigade in North Tipperary 1917–1921; Part II*
Sharkey, Neil, *The Third Tipperary Brigade – A Photographic Record*

Tipperary Historical Journal 1995
Kinnane, Paddy, *My Part in the War of Independence*

Tipperary Historical Journal 1996
Kinnane, Paddy, *My Part in the War of Independence Part 2*

Tipperary Historical Journal 1998
Sharkey, Seán, *My Role as an Intelligence Officer with the Third Tipperary Brigade (1919-1921)*
Maher, Jim, *Dan Breen looks back 50 years from 1967.*

Tipperary Historical Journal 2004
Crowe, Tadgh, *Life with a Flying Column, 1919-1921*

Tipperary Historical Journal 2005
Merrigan, Paul, *Life with the South Tipperary Volunteers 1914-1921*

Tipperary Historical Journal 2006
Patterson, Tony, *Third Tipperary Brigade, Number Two Flying Column, January to June 1921.*

Capuchin Annual; Dublin, 1969
Hayes, Michael, *The Importance of Dáil Éireann*
Kavanagh, Seán, *The Irish Volunteers' Intelligence Organisation*
Mulcahy, Richard, *Chief of Staff*

The Dublin Review, No. 12.
Ferriter, Diarmaid, *In Such Deadly Earnest*

The Nationalist Clonmel, 1890-1990
Clonmel and the Rising of 1916 by Frank Drohan

Tipperary Deputies in the Second Dáil

Past & Present, May, 1996
English, Richard, *The inborn hate of things English: Ernie O'Malley and the Irish Revolution 1916–1923*

Canadian Journal of History, April, 2003
Leeson, David, *Death in the afternoon: The Croke Park Massacre, 21 November 1920.*

Acknowledgements

The sections of this book dealing with the Young Irelanders and the Fenians in Tipperary owe everything to the original research undertaken by Patrick C. Power in his entertaining and erudite *History of South Tipperary*. Much of the research on Michael Doheny was done by Michael O'Donnell for a lecture whose text I have the benefit of reading on fethard.com. David Leeson's original research into British archives is taken advantage of in the chapter dealing with Bloody Sunday.

I consulted the Bureau of Military History documents in Dublin's National Archives, and am grateful to the staff there for their patience and kindness. I'm especially appreciative of the encouragement of Michael Murphy, my sisters Gerardine and Caroline, their husbands Eamonn O'Meara and Val Needham, my brother Robbie, and my nephew James Needham.

Colleagues, friends, co-conspirators, assistants, usual suspects, and collaborators have included Jocelyn and Lucy Bradell, Dan Stuart, Mike Luongo, Gerry O'Boyle at The Boogaloo, Carwyn Ellis, Elaine Palmer, Marek Pytel, Maki Kita, The Brink, Anne Foley, Seb Tennant, Spencer Kansa, David Kerekes at Headpress, Matt Willis, Mattia Zaparello, www.thehandstand.net, Daniel Figgis, Deirdre Behan, The Master Musicians of Joujouka, Shane Cullen, Shane O'Reilly, Gerry Ambrose, Peter Berresford Ellis, *An*

Phoblacht, Frank Callanan, Dennis McClean, Brendan Maher at *Start* magazine, South Tipperary Arts Centre, Marie Boland and her staff at Clonmel Library, Ulick O'Connor, Prof. Liam Kennedy at Queen's, Brian Ronan, Patrick Crowley, Catherine Twibill and Mary Feehan at Mercier Press, Tavis Henry, Henderson Downing, Tipp FM, Paul Lamont at outsideleft.com, Tav Falco, Chuck Prophet, *Tipperary Star*, Paul Hawkins for sticking to his guns, Hamri the Painter of Morocco, Tiago Almeida, Chris Campion, Shevaun Wilder, Malcolm Kelly, Anna Lanigan, Seán Dowling, Pat Norris, Josie Heffernan, Jimmy Norris, Tom and Joan Ambrose, Michael and Deirdre Ahearn, Ernie Hogan, Kirk Lake, John Foley, Carrie Acheson, Martin Mansergh, Nana Spring, *The Nationalist*, myspace/chelseahotelmanhattan, Brendan Long, Martin Arthur, Fintan Deere, and William Corbett.

My gratitude goes out to An t-Athair Colmcille Conway, the *Tipperary Historical Journal*, Marcus Bourke, Liam O'Duibhir, Michael Ahearn, and all of the other Tipperary historians without whom I would be lost. Frank Rynne procured some vital information for me, as did Des Farrell.

Finally, the author and publisher would like to thank Martin O'Dwyer for his kind permission to reproduce some of the photographs in this work.

INDEX